A Tale of Five Cities
& Other Memoirs

Novels by Joyce Elbert

A Martini on the Other Table (1963)
The Crazy Ladies (1969)
The Goddess Hangup (1970)
Getting Rid of Richard (1972)
Drunk in Madrid (1972)
The Three of Us (1973)
The Crazy Lovers (1976)
A Very Cagey Lady (1980)
Red Eye Blues (1981)
The Return of the Crazy Ladies (1984)

A Tale of Five Cities
& Other Memoirs

Joyce Elbert

Tough Poets Press
Arlington, Massachusetts

Copyright © 2022 by the Literary Estate of Joyce Elbert

Cover photo of the author by David Attie

All rights reserved including the right to reproduce
this book or parts thereof in any form.

ISBN 978-0-578-39241-7

Tough Poets Press
Arlington, Massachusetts 02476
U.S.A.

www.toughpoets.com

Contents

FOREWORD BY ERJE AYDEN 1

MOVIES: 1934 3
ROOMING HOUSE: 1955 21
FIRST NOVEL: 1956 47

A TALE OF FIVE CITIES

ACAPULCO: 1954 71
PARIS: 1959 99
CAMPELLO: 1973 145
LONDON: 1973 171
MARTHA'S VINEYARD: 1984 201

ABOUT THE AUTHOR 223

ACKNOWLEDGMENTS 225

Foreword

ONE CHILLY APRIL EVENING in 1965 I dropped by Frank O'Hara's studio for a quick shot of bourbon. As I was leaving Frank asked me if I was going back to the Chelsea Hotel where I lived. I said yes.

"Erje, Larry is visiting a friend there. Do you mind if I give you a package to take to him?"

"Of course not."

I didn't know Larry Rivers well except that I was familiar with his canvases and I knew that he was very close friends with Frank.

After a few pleasantries Larry questioned me.

"Do you only write short stories? Have you ever read Joyce Elbert?"

"No, I'm into novels now. I'm sorry, but I don't know who Joyce Elbert is."

"A very good short story writer. You should read her. You'd like her."

Anyway, a few days later I was visiting with Seymour Krim in his East 10th Street apartment, I remembered Joyce Elbert.

"Seymour, who's Joyce Elbert? Do you know her?"

"She's a friend of mine and a very good writer. Why?"

"Nothing. A few days ago Larry Rivers mentioned her name and said I should read her."

"And you should. You'd like her writing. She is as good as Flannery O'Connor. Do you want to meet her?"

"No."

Seymour went to his file cabinet and brought out a typewritten manuscript

"Here, Erje, Joyce Elbert. Read it and bring it back."

1

It never surprised me when Seymour pulled out original manuscripts by writers from Joseph Heller to Hubert Selby.

The next day Seymour called me at home.

"What do you think?"

"About what, Seymour?"

"About Joyce Elbert."

"She's good. She *is* as good as Flannery O'Connor."

"You sure you don't want to meet her? She's a character."

"I'm sure, Seymour."

I met Joyce Elbert four years later. Through the years we became great friends. It helped, too, that my then-wife Patricia liked her as much as I did. Joyce was fun. A terrific friend.

I could write a lot about Joyce, but I won't because she's a very private person. I respect her privacy.

But I'd like to say a word or two about her writing. She's one of the best because she is all ears and all imagination. She doesn't judge her characters when she writes. She tries to understand them as humanly as possible and her sense of humor is priceless—and to the point.

Erje Ayden
(Author of *The Crazy Green of Second Avenue, Confessions of a Nowaday Child, Sadness at Leaving,* etc.)

Movies: 1934

MY MOTHER started taking me to the movies that winter, little suspecting the powerful impact they would have on my life. The first movie I ever saw starred bouncy Shirley Temple singing, "The Good Ship Lollipop." According to Twentieth Century Fox, to whom she was under contract, their remarkable child prodigy was four years old.

"Just think," my mother wistfully said as we took our seats. "She's the same age as you."

Only much later did I discover that Twentieth Century Fox had lied. Shirley was six at the time. Only much later than that did I discover that their lie was mild compared to the lies of illusion I had absorbed from a multitude of celluloid images, year after year after year. Like other moviegoers of my generation, I was subjected to a grave distortion of truth right from the start. For example, all around me in "real life" were signs of shabbily dressed people looking bereft and miserable during the Great Depression, while up there in "reel life" were signs of elegantly dressed people being witty and carefree, enjoying themselves to the hilt.

As if that weren't confusing enough, the former was taking place in dingy washed out colors while the latter was in glittering black and white with lively, upbeat music. Anyone would have been bamboozled by such conflicting messages, let alone an impressionable child whose mother failed to provide any insight into the situation. When I asked her why we didn't live in a big house with white staircases and black servants like people in the movie we had just seen, she said, "Those houses belong to rich people and we're not rich."

"Why not?"

"Because your father lost his money."

"Where did he lose it? On the subway?"

That made her smile. "No, on a place called Wall Street. It happened before you were born."

It seemed extremely careless of him. "Maybe if he tried, he could get it back."

"I'm afraid not, darling. Your father's money is gone forever."

"Why didn't the people in the movie lose their money, too?"

"That's what I'd like to know," my mother said.

Neither of us cared for what would later come to be known as the "slice of life" movies starring such actors as Edward G. Robinson, George Raft, James Cagney and John Garfield. They were grim and joyless, their only appeal being the depiction of people in worse circumstances than ours, but we went anyway. We went twice a week to whatever was playing because it beat spending the afternoon in our three room apartment, watching WPA workers off in the distance (one of my uncles among them) erect what would eventually become my high school. As far as I was concerned, going to the movies beat anything we could have possibly done.

We always went to the first show at noon and to this day I can't bear to see a movie after dark. Our local movie palace, The Allerton, was a ten minute walk from where we lived in a remote section of the northeast Bronx and my mother unfailingly took along a sandwich for herself, having fed me beforehand. An indelible memory is of watching the credits roll for a Busby Berkeley musical starring Dick Powell while hearing my mother discreetly chewing her egg salad, lettuce and tomato extravaganza, with a pickle slice on the side. I used to wish she would do this before we left home, but she never found the time.

Or maybe she had unconsciously clued into the syndrome of a future generation who would watch TV and eat their TV dinners alone, lonely souls, all. My mother certainly was, my company notwithstanding. I suspect she went to the movies twice a week because she didn't know what hit her. Nothing in her life had emotionally prepared her for marriage or motherhood and yet there she was, trapped, with no hope in sight. Before marrying my father she worked in a factory as a millinery copyist and apparently enjoyed it, since whenever she spoke about those days it was with great enthusiasm. Most of her co-workers had been Cuban girls who taught her the words of popular Spanish songs, which she still occasionally sung in a clear first soprano voice. "Amapola" was her favorite. Although she never said it in so many words, I would later get the distinct impression that marriage held no interest for her and she had only succumbed to her own mother's pressure at the then-late age of twenty-five.

My father was considered a good catch as he had money, and my mother's family didn't. That my mother didn't care about money or material possessions seemed beside the point. What she did care about was pleasing my grandmother who was afraid her only daughter would be an old maid. Unfortunately the marriage took place in 1929. Less than a year later my father was not only dead broke, but he had cracked up from the shock of finding his once-thriving dress manufacturing company bankrupt. Then I came howling into the world.

No wonder my mother started dragging me to the double features as soon as she could. While she was fond of my father, I doubt if she was ever romantically in love with him the way Barbara Stanwyck, Loretta Young or Irene Dunne were in love with their dashing leading men. My parents' temperaments were very different and they had little in common. If my father hadn't found movies the ultimate bore, the gap between them might have been bridged somewhat but his form of escape was gin rummy, which he played incessantly with his cronies during non-working hours.

Every so often my mother would succeed in coaxing him to the Allerton Theatre on Tuesday night, which was dish night. Each person who bought a ticket received one free plate (or cup, saucer, bowl) from a gold rimmed dinner service of forty. Those enterprising souls who made a practice of flocking to the Allerton every Tuesday night eventually wound up owning the entire set. It irritated my mother that even with this extra incentive, my father not only resisted going but would doze off a few minutes after the movie started.

"How can you fall asleep when Joan Crawford is on the screen?" she would ask him afterward.

"How can you stay awake?"

His make believe was not hers and she had no female support system to turn to for solace. Having been born and brought up in Brooklyn, which was a long subway ride away, my mother hadn't yet made any friends in the neighborhood. She had no sisters, her mother had died the previous year, so she was pretty much alone. The isolation must have been overwhelming, particularly since we didn't get a telephone until many years later. I remember a dark cloud descending upon us as we left the Allerton and began walking home. Gone was smiling, debonair Douglas Fairbanks, Jr. and about to return was my defeated father, tired from standing on his feet all day and then pushing into a crowded subway for a one-hour ride back to where he had started early that morning.

Not that I ever heard either of my parents complain. It might have been better for all concerned had they aired their grievances, but instead they silently and stoically made the best of their lot. My father would often sit in our darkened living room after dinner, watching an electric fire in the Art Deco fireplace, not saying anything. After my mother washed and dried the dishes, she remained in the kitchen to iron. Those were the days before synthetics and I guess she felt compelled to iron her beautiful silk and satin undies (gifts from my father before Wall Street "laid an egg," as *Variety* so quaintly put it), along with more prosaic items like sheets and pillowcases. Sometimes when she finished the three of us would listen to a radio program, but by ten o'clock it was lights out with the alarm set for seven a.m. I used to drift off to sleep still dreaming about the stars I had watched earlier on the glittering black and white screen.

This routine went on for two years.

"You're a big girl now," my mother said one morning. "You don't have to go to the movies anymore. You'll be going to school."

No more movies? I felt devastated, betrayed. As a result I developed such an instant hatred for school that I began throwing up every weekday morning in anticipation of the ordeal. Finally the principal told my mother I was too high-strung for classroom teaching. I asked her what that meant.

"It means you're an overly sensitive, overly imaginative child. The principal thinks you would do better studying at home, at least for the first term." She glanced at the clock. "We're going to have to rush if we want to make the new Deanna Durbin musical."

My relief must have been apparent because she added, "Don't think I'm going to keep you home indefinitely. This is just a temporary arrangement."

"How will I learn to read and write?"

"I'll teach you."

Every morning we had our lessons and twice a week at noon we went to the movies. I felt happy again with things back to normal, but in due course I had to take a reading and comprehension test, which I passed with flying colors and so entered second grade. I didn't like school any more than before, yet by then I had become resigned to my fate. Besides, I figured that in a few more years I would be old enough to go to the movies by myself on Saturday afternoons and when I turned eleven my mother gave me permission to do just that.

At first, I went with some of my girlfriends only to discover that they talked after the movie started. Even worse, they expected me to answer them. Although I begged for quiet, they couldn't hold their tongues longer than a couple of minutes. My mother might have eaten egg salad sandwiches, but she never spoke once the lights had dimmed for fear of missing a star's single word or gesture. To her, the Hollywood product was deserving of respect and piety. To me, too.

"Gee, Joyce. It's only a movie," one friend grumbled after I had shut her up for the umpteenth time.

Only a movie? I found her irreverence shocking, appalling, still it made me realize that to her and the others movies were just another place to kill time (like the local ice cream parlor) whereas to me they represented a world of fantasy and romance that I had become hooked on. After that I went to the Allerton by myself and over the next eight years I rarely missed a week without seeing at least two of Hollywood's newest releases. (This amounted to over eight hundred movies, I later calculated.) I also devoured popular magazines like *Photoplay* and *Modern Screen*, which devoted themselves to behind-the-scenes stories of glamorous stars leading exciting lives as shown in the sepia-toned pictures. I couldn't wait for the next issue to hit the stands any more than I could wait for the next movie to arrive at the Allerton Theatre.

I was utterly fascinated by the stars and the characters they portrayed on screen, but tended to get the two mixed up. Sometimes I wondered if Norma Shearer and Robert Taylor were really acting or if their true identities had somehow become entangled with those of the people they pretended to be. Where did one stop and the other begin? It was a question that haunted me for years. Faces of the stars haunted me, as well. In those days, no two looked even remotely alike. My favorites were Ginger Rogers and Fred Astaire. When they danced the Carioca, I forgot that I came from an unhappy family living in uncertain times.

With so many millions of people out of work in the Thirties, my father was considered extremely fortunate to have a job. Some of the men who lost their money in the Crash jumped out the window, others eventually went back into business. My father chose a third course. He had a craft that was in demand on Seventh Avenue and after recovering from his nervous breakdown, he swore he would never again run his own company. The risk was too great. Determined to play it safe from then on, he took a job as cutter and pattern maker for women's medium-priced dresses. His salary was thirty-five dollars a week.

How my mother managed to put anything aside for luxuries I

will never know but when I was eight she told me I had a choice between taking piano lessons or dancing lessons. "Which one do you prefer?" she asked.

Learning how to play the piano seemed an almost impossible task as I was practically tone-deaf, but learning how to dance appealed to me a lot. In addition to Ginger and Fred, I had been bowled over by the tap-dancing prowess of Shirley Temple, Eleanor Powell, Ruby Keeler and Ann Miller. My mother enrolled me in a nearby school headed by a Miss Azzarella who put on semi-annual shows to prove to parents how talented their offspring had become under her tutelage. Miss Azzarella was a tall scrawny woman with long narrow feet, not unlike my own. I watched in fascination as those feet went through the motions of the basic time-step plus a few fanciful variations, convinced I would never be able to imitate her. I was wrong. Miss Azzarella told my mother that I was a natural dancer.

"Joyce might even want to make a career out of it," she added to my mother's surprise and irritation. (My mother was determined that I become a schoolteacher even though I told her in no uncertain terms that never in a million years would that happen.) "Now," Miss Azzarella said, "we have to work on her singing."

Most people laughed when I tried to sing. I was an alto—loud, flat, terrible—and had long since given up hope of ever sounding any better.

"In music class, the teacher always asks her to keep quiet," my mother said.

"We'll see about *that*," Miss Azzarella sniffed. She then asked me to warble a few bars of "Franklin D. Roosevelt Jones," without music. It was a disaster but Miss Azzarella was undeterred. She sat down at the piano and struck up the opening notes. "I know you can sing on key if I accompany you. Come on, dear, make an effort."

With great trepidation, I gave it a try. Then I tried again. And with Miss Azzarello's unflagging encouragement, again and again. "You see? You're improving already! We have to keep working on your voice so you'll be in top form for the big show next month."

My stomach turned over. "I thought all I would be doing was dancing."

"No, dear, you'll be singing too."

Who, me? The worst singer at P.S. 86? I found it hard to believe, but as the weeks went by even my mother had to admit that I was making progress. My confidence began to swell and I had visions of bringing down the house as I belted out a medley of tunes while tapping energetically from one end of the stage to the other. In order to ensure my success, I began practicing in my spare time at home. When the neighbors beneath us complained of the noise, my mother took me to the basement where I wouldn't disturb anyone. Before long I had started to think of myself as a double threat entertainer, not unlike Shirley Temple at her most winsome. The closer we got to the day of the big show, the more anxious I became about which solo number I would be asked to perform. I was hoping for "A-Tisket, A-Tasket," because the song was clearly Miss Azzarello's favorite and I felt sure she would devise a special tap routine to go along with it, as well as an outstanding costume. Finally we were all lined up to hear our fates. My knees were shaking so badly I was certain everyone could hear them.

"Joyce, Janet and Joan." Miss Azzarella beckoned to me and two of my classmates. "Please step forward."

We did so, curiously.

"I've decided to make you girls an act," she announced. "I'm calling you 'The Three J's' and you will sing the 'Good Morning' number. Janet will stand in the middle because she's the tallest."

It was the greatest disappointment I had suffered in my eight and a half years. Not only wouldn't I be doing a solo, I wouldn't even be in the middle! What's more, I knew that Joan and Janet could outsing me any day of the week as they were first sopranos with perfect pitch. The thought of being overshadowed by them filled me with dread. Rage. Resentment. My only consolation was that I could outdance the two klutzes. I was faster, livelier, more sure of my timing. Still the indignity of having to share the spotlight plagued me during rehearsals, as did the high pure voices of my teammates. I prayed they would both come down with laryngitis so I could have the stage to myself. Wasn't that what happened to Ruby Keeler, more or less, in one of her movies?

"What are you so nervous about?" my mother asked the morning of the show.

"Sounding like a fool compared to Joan and Janet."

"Don't be silly. Since the three of you will be singing in unison, nobody will realize they're better than you."

"I don't want to sing in unison! I want to be a solo act!"

"But if you were, then everyone would know you had a terrible voice," my mother patiently replied. "This way, Joan and Janet will cover for you."

When we arrived at the makeshift theatre, I saw that the two klutzes were radiantly healthy with no sign of laryngitis. We wore matching pink and gold organdy dresses, pink tap shoes, pink socks, and gold hair ribbons. While the act before us was doing its number, I peeked out through the curtains at a crowded anticipatory audience. My parents, my uncle Nat in from San Francisco, and my best friend Gloria Gittelman were in the front row awaiting my debut. I thought I would die of stage fright until I heard the musicians strike up the opening bars of our song.

"Our next number, 'Good Morning,' will be performed by the Three J's," Miss Azzarella exuberantly announced on the loudspeaker. "And here they are!"

Something came over me then, probably four years of double features at the Allerton Theatre. "I have to be in the middle," I cried, elbowing a startled Janet out of the way.

"But she's the tallest," Joan whimpered.

I stubbornly positioned myself between them. "So what?"

"Get back where you belong," Miss Azzarella hissed.

It was too late. Weeks of strict rehearsal had trained us not to miss our cue and out to center stage we went, dancing and singing as though nothing were amiss. Having thrust myself in the spotlight, I felt imbued with a new sense of destiny and realized that my voice was even more deafening than usual. In fact it completely drowned out the sweet soprano voices of my two teammates, note after ear-splitting note.

> Good morning, good morning
> We've danced the whole night through
> Good morning, good morning
> To you! And you! And you!

I was dancing with more frenetic energy than I had ever displayed before, a big theatrical smile frozen on my face, hardly aware of my partners except when I caught their fleeting glances of shock and disbelief. In the front row Gloria Gittelman was laughing hysterically while my father and uncle Nat were smiling. Only my mother looked disturbed, but not even she could dim my high spirits. When the number ended, I felt flushed with triumph and took an extra bow to loud applause. Once backstage Joan burst into tears and Janet said she hated me.

"You're mean and selfish," she cried, punching me in the stomach. "I never want to speak to you again."

I kicked her in the shins. "You're just jealous because I stole the show."

"You can't even sing." She scratched my arm with surprisingly sharp nails. "You're a Listener."

I slapped her across the face. "I was singing today, stupid, and dancing better than either of you two elephants."

"You call that singing? You were screeching." She tore at my hair. "I have perfect pitch and so does Joan, but nobody could hear us. It's your fault and don't call me stupid, you moron."

I bit her wrist, wondering if this had ever happened to Eleanor Powell or Ann Miller. "I'll call you anything I like and for your information, I am not a Listener."

"Listener! Listener! Listener!"

I ran into the dressing room to escape her next attack and put a Band-Aid on my bleeding arm, imagining the day I would have a real dressing room of my own with a red star on the door, bouquets of flowers all around.

"Miss Azzarella is furious with you," my mother said when she arrived, a frown on her face. "She thinks you planned to switch places in advance so you could get the better of Joan and Janet. That's not true, is it?"

"I didn't plan anything. It just happened. How did I sound?"

"Loud. They must have heard you in Canarsie. Miss Azzarella said you might as well have been doing a solo act."

After that I began tap dancing in the subway whenever my parents and I went anywhere. My father found these performances highly amusing, but my mother was mortified to see me go into a fast time-step as I belted out refrains of a popular song while passengers threw nickels and dimes at me. I picked up the money and kept on tapping, often into the next car. Sometimes I played the entire train, wondering whether a famous Hollywood producer was riding the subway and would sign me to a seven-year contract. As I waited for the good news to descend, bad news arrived. My dancing school was going out of business. Heartbroken, I tried to prevail on my mother to enroll me in another school but she refused.

"There isn't anything else nearby and I'm not taking the subway to Queens or Manhattan." She saw the tears roll down my cheeks. "Besides, it's not as though you were going to make a career out of singing and dancing."

"*How do you know?*" I sobbed.

"Don't be silly, Joyce. Without music, you can't even carry a tune."

At the age of nine, my life was over. "I'll bet Shirley Temple can't either."

With my career as an entertainer scuttled, I turned my dubious talents to drawing pictures of movie stars. Bing Crosby had recently become my favorite and I drew his portrait in crayon, then in watercolor. It wasn't as easy as I had imagined and by the time I completed a fairly good likeness, I had gone through fifteen sheets of paper. The only reason I saved the rejects was in order to rate my progress as I went along, but just as I was about to throw them away my mother stopped me.

"We'll hang these in the kitchen," she said, choosing the best of the lot. "Over the table."

I was horrified. "But they're no good. They were only for practice."

"They're very good. I'm impressed. Do you want to be a painter someday?"

"No, I want to be a singer and dancer."

"Let's not get started on that fantasy again." She found a few thumbtacks and began pinning my rejects to the bare white wall. "See? They really perk up the room."

"No, they don't. They make Bing Crosby look like a goofball."

When my father came home, he stared at my handiwork, perplexed. "Who is that man over the kitchen table and why is he wearing lipstick?"

"I told you they were terrible," I said to my mother.

She ignored me. "If you went to the movies more often, Charlie, you would recognize Bing Crosby when you saw him. Doesn't Joyce have talent?"

My father winked at me. "In the subway, that's where she has talent."

After that I painted Betty Grable, Don Ameche, Judy Garland, Clark Gable, Lana Turner, John Garfield, Ann Sheridan, Spencer Tracy and Hedy Lamarr. There was no stopping me and yet the more I drew, the more I could see that I had no flair for it which only egged me on to draw still more in hopes of improving my skills. In time, however, I began to realize those hopes were in vain.

Not so my mother who had hung my creations in every nook and cranny of our small apartment, even the insides of closets, so that wherever I turned there was another movie star smiling at me with some glaring physical defect. Betty Grable was cross-eyed. John Garfield's nose resembled a potato. Spencer Tracy had chicken pox. Hedy Lamarr looked like Dracula, etcetera. It was very depressing and I waited for an evening when my parents were out, then I ripped all the drawings off the walls and threw them in the trash.

My mother was chagrined. "Years from now when you're a successful artist, you'll be sorry you didn't save those pictures."

"No, I won't because I'm through with painting. I'm going to be a writer." I had just seen *The Barretts of Wimpole Street*, which chronicled the life of Elizabeth Barrett Browning. "Probably a poet."

"First it was a tap dancer, then a painter, now a poet." My mother turned to my father in despair. "Where does she get these ideas?"

"Don't ask me, Melba. It's your side of the family that's crazy."

I had been badgering my mother to let me go to the movies in the West Bronx and when I turned thirteen she finally agreed. This was a major concession on her part and it made me feel very grown-up since unlike the good old Allerton Theatre, which was within walking distance of home, I would be taking a crosstown bus, albeit in daytime, and entering a much more sophisticated milieu. Compared to our hayseed neighborhood, filled with fields of daisies and long stretches of empty land, the West Bronx was densely populated, bustling, affluent. In the past I had gone there with my mother to shop at Alexander's Department Store and it was the next best thing to Manhattan. People in the West Bronx considered themselves superior to us. They were the city slickers, we were the hicks. (A mile from where I lived, families kept goats.)

"There's a condition," my mother said. "You have to take one of your girlfriends with you. I don't want you going alone."

"Can we have lunch out? At Child's?"

"If you'd like."

My cup had definitely runneth over. I asked Gloria Gittelman to join me, but she had to attend a cousin's bar mitzvah. My next two choices were also unavailable and I had to settle for Frances Zahler, a sallow-faced girl with a nervous disposition. When Saturday rolled around, I tried to hide my excitement as we boarded the bus and paid our nickel fare. We were dressed in our best clothes and wore small patent leather shoulder bags containing the money we would need, as well as a fresh handkerchief and a comb. The money amounted to little more than a few dollars, yet it seemed like a fortune to me.

"Do you know what you're going to order at Child's?" Frances whispered as we zipped along Fordham Road past the famous Jesuit college. She was clutching her shoulder bag for dear life. "I've never ordered lunch at a restaurant."

"I'll know when we get there."

"Will I know, too?"

"Of course you will," I said with a false certainty.

At Child's we were seated by a pretty hostess who handed us the menus. Another first. After much deliberation, I ordered the chicken croquettes, mashed potatoes, and cole slaw. Frances did the same.

"Would you girls like something to drink?" the waitress asked.

"Lemonade, please," I said.

"What makes you think I wanted lemonade?" Frances demanded a few seconds later. "Maybe I wanted ginger ale."

"Why didn't you say so?"

"You didn't give me a chance."

"I'm sorry, but I didn't want to look indecisive."

"What does that mean?"

"Like I've never done this before."

"You haven't."

"That's not the point!"

"Why are you getting so angry?"

I regretted having taken Frances Zahler along on this adventure. She clearly wasn't up to it. "Stop acting like such a baby. Start acting more mature."

"I don't feel mature." She seemed about to cry. "I feel nervous."

"Look, Frances, we're going to have a nice lunch and then we're going to walk across the street and see *A Star is Born*." It was the original version with Janet Gaynor and Frederic March, which I had somehow missed when it first came out. "Then we're going to take the bus home. What's there to be nervous about?"

"I think my Aunt Tillie with the red hair is coming to visit."

"That's impossible. She visited you only two weeks ago."

"No, she didn't. You're thinking of Gloria's Aunt Tillie."

"I am not. I distinctly remember you saying that your Aunt Tillie would be here shortly." It was our secret code for getting one's period.

"Then she's come twice in one month." Frances's lips were trembling. "Does it mean that I'm going to bleed to death?"

At that moment our lunch arrived, but I felt too distracted to eat. "Maybe you should go to the ladies room and check," I said.

"I'm afraid to move. What if the back of my dress is stained?"

"You would feel it if your Aunt Tillie was here, wouldn't you?"

"Not necessarily. She's very sneaky, especially the first day."

"Why don't you stand up so I can take a look?"

Frances was appalled. "In the middle of a crowded restaurant? With everyone watching?"

"Nobody is paying any attention to us and we're not in the middle, we're on the side. Come on, just do it."

She hesitantly got to her feet and turned around. Sure enough, on the back of her dress was a bright pink spot the size of a quarter.

"Your Aunt Tillie must really love you. She's here again."

Turning beet red, Frances plopped down in her chair. "How will I get out of here? I've never been so embarrassed in my life. What am I going to do? Say something!"

"*Bringing Up Baby*."

"What?"

"It's a movie with Katharine Hepburn and Cary Grant. When they're in a restaurant her dress accidentally gets ripped in back revealing her panties, but Cary Grant comes to the rescue. He positions himself directly behind her and that's how they walk out, with him covering the rip. I will do the same for you, Frances." I felt very pleased with this ingenious solution. "It was a very funny scene."

"*Funny?* You call what's happening to me *funny?*" She began to cry into her mashed potatoes. "I should never have agreed to come here today. I don't even like the movies. Besides, where am I going to buy a Kotex? They don't sell them at the candy counter, you know."

"We'll stop at a drugstore." I wondered why actresses never got their period in the movies. I hadn't thought about that before, but it was an interesting question.

"How will I attach the Kotex? I don't have my belt."

"Just stuff it in your panties and stop whining. It will be fine until you get home."

"It's easy for you to talk," she said, spitefully. "I'll bet you wouldn't be thrilled if your Aunt Tillie showed up at an inconvenient time—and twice in a month at that."

Her bad humor was starting to get on my nerves. We finished lunch, made as dignified an exit as possible, bought the Kotex, and paid for our movie tickets. Then the lights dimmed and the screen lit up. Although sniveling Frances Zahler was seated beside me, for the next two hours she might as well have been in Singapore. *A Star is Born* was the story of one woman's professional triumph marred by personal heartbreak and as far as I was concerned, the most engrossing movie I had ever seen. I identified completely with poor little Esther Blodgett (played by Janet Gaynor), a young aspiring actress who goes on to Hollywood fame and fortune while her once famous husband, Norman Maine (played by Frederic March) goes on to alcoholic defeat and finally death by suicide.

The last emotion-packed scene was too much for me. When Esther Blodgett comes out of seclusion to attend a mobbed movie premiere it is after her beloved husband has killed himself so as not to continue to be a burden and embarrassment to her. Fans clamor for the glamorous star to speak. She takes the microphone, there is a moment's hesitation, then—

"This is *Mrs.* Norman Maine," she proudly declares.

I burst into uncontrollable tears. Even Frances was surprised. "What's wrong?" she asked. "Did your Aunt Tillie show up, too?"

Over the next few years, the movies helped me blossom into an attractive and knowledgeable teenager. I learned how to kiss by watching Linda Darnell and Lana Turner do it. I learned how to swim the backstroke by copying Esther Williams in her poolside extravaganzas. I learned how to dance the Lindy by imitating Betty Hutton. I learned how to put my hair in an upsweep compliments of Ann Sheridan. I learned how to flirt thanks to Elizabeth Taylor. I learned how to make men crawl from Gloria Graham. I learned how to be a *femme fatale* by taking lessons from Gene Tierney.

I also learned how to switch roles as the occasion demanded so I could go from cute and bouncy (June Allyson) to cool and serene (Grace Kelly) to tough and bitchy (Joan Bennett), without missing a beat. I learned about men, loves conquers all and happily ever after from the movies. I learned that there were good women and bad women, good men and bad men, and very little in between (except for Eve Arden). What confused me was that the bad women and bad men had all the fun until the end of the movie when suddenly they were forced to pay the consequences. Often this abrupt plot turn happened within seconds, whereas the fun had lasted for almost two hours. It was easy to forget the punishment and remember the fireworks. It was easy to conclude that being a bad woman seemed thrilling, but being a good woman seemed tedious and boring.

If I had any doubts, all I had to do was observe my mother and her friends plow through their daily routine wearing their drab housedresses. When I grew up, I would be a bad woman and get to parade around in gorgeous clothes and kiss handsome, unscrupulous men. Not even the sight of Joan Crawford in a prison uniform (meticulously tailored to flatter her slim figure) could deter me. I was no dope. I knew she would soon be out on parole and return to her furs, slinky gowns and exciting reign of debauchery.

By the time I turned nineteen, I realized that the Joan Crawford persona was too limited, masochistic, and humorless to want to emulate. I also dispensed with cute, bouncy, cool, serene, tough and bitchy as being irrelevant for what I wished to achieve: irresistible glamour coupled with outstanding professional success.

Eventually I evolved into a watered down combination of sultry Rita Hayworth who lived for her man and feisty Rosalind Russell who lived for her career. While aware that such a package had never existed in movie lore and would undoubtedly deter the average man, I felt sure it would not stop my Prince Charming when he came along. It didn't but only because I was so bowled over by him that the Rosalind Russell side of me took a fast nosedive, leaving the vulnerable Rita Hayworth facsimile whom he fell in love with and married.

For the next few years I fought like hell to restore the missing component and make my husband see what a gifted writer I was. I worked very hard at it and like Janet Gaynor in *A Star is Born* eventually beat him at his own game, even though it wasn't my intention any more than it had been Esther Blodgett's. I became a more successful writer than him so naturally my professional triumph was marred by personal heartbreak, albeit long after we were divorced. Like Frederic March in the movie, my husband committed suicide and while it wasn't by walking into the Pacific Ocean, it was suicide nonetheless.

When I heard about it, I remembered that long ago Saturday afternoon in the West Bronx with Frances Zahler and how I had sobbed during the last scene of *A Star is Born*. Having wondered why that movie had such a profound emotional effect on me, now I knew: it eerily foreshadowed events in my own life. Or had I led my life to fit the seductive script without realizing it? Who can say? Still I will never know whether things would have turned out differently if my mother hadn't started taking me to the movies when I was four years old.

Rooming House: 1955

I MOVED into the rooming house on an overcast day in October after I had been forced out of the apartment I was subletting from friends. Not sure where to go and not having much money, I checked into a cheap hotel until I realized that even that was beyond my means. Then I found the rooming house. A sprawling five story structure called Irving Place Court, it was located on East 19th Street off 4th Avenue before it became known as Park Avenue South. Irving Place Court had a small switchboard in the vestibule and seemed very clean with pale gray walls and shiny linoleum floors.

"It will cost you fifteen dollars a week plus tax, payable in advance." The manager, a saturnine man named Al, looked me over sharply. "No cooking in your room, no smoking in bed, no overnight guests, *capish?*"

I was given a square corner room with a private toilet and for bathing a windowless room a few feet outside my door. There was no shower, only a tub. Opposite the tub was a wide shelf on which I was about to put soap and toothpaste when I realized it would easily hold my borrowed rotisserie (the precursor to toaster ovens). Al may have warned me not to cook in my room, but he hadn't said anything about the bathroom. Feeling quite ingenious, I decided to use the top of the rotisserie to heat water for coffee in the morning while I warmed up a corn muffin inside. That the muffin would turn on a spit meant for a chicken made me laugh for the first time since finding myself homeless, but my amusement was short-lived. As soon as I switched on the rotisserie, it blew a fuse and all the lights on the floor went out. I stood there plunged in darkness, feeling like a criminal, while outraged cries filled the hallway.

"Who the hell overloaded the circuits?"

"Where are the fuse boxes?"

"What kind of cheap dump is this, anyway?"

I hoped that if I didn't move and didn't breathe, Al might never learn of my insubordination. Apparently he didn't because a few minutes later the lights went back on and I wasn't crucified. Then I saw my mistake. I had turned the rotisserie to the "high" setting. The next morning I tried "low" and crossed my fingers. Success. No fuses blew but it took over an hour for the water in my tiny saucepan to come to a boil, by which time the corn muffin had burned to a crisp. The solution seemed obvious. Get up earlier, put the muffin in later.

Even though I had noticed some of my neighbors scurrying down to 4th Avenue in the early hours to buy sweet rolls and plastic containers of coffee at the corner deli, I wasn't about to follow their lead. With my life in such a state of upheaval, I guess it was only natural to cling to any kind of creature comfort, however small, and not having to rush out while I was still half asleep seemed very important. I even bought a small tray at Woolworth to put the coffee and corn muffin on, so I could pretend that a loving husband had brought me breakfast in bed.

Because I had no refrigerator, I kept a quarter pound of butter on the window ledge and although it never spoiled, one windy night it flew away. Although my disappointment was profound, I decided I would have to do without butter and put a jar of blueberry jam in the bathing room. Individual cans of grapefruit juice, a box of corn muffins and some instant coffee—all smuggled in under my raincoat—completed the breakfast larder.

Every morning while waiting for the tub to fill up, I would drink a glass of grapefruit juice, dump some instant coffee in a mug and watch the corn muffin go round. When I finished bathing, I wrapped myself in a terry robe and turned off the rotisserie. Since mine was a corner room, no other tenant walked past me and I reveled in being able to take my breakfast back to bed to sip and munch while I thought about how I had ended up in such a sorry state.

When I left my husband, John Elbert, I did just that. I left. Walked out and never came back. Twice. Meaning I not only gave him the apartment we had shared on Thompson Street, but also the ground floor apartment on West 10th Street that I subsequently sublet from actor friends who were touring with *The Solid Gold Cadillac*. If my actions sound altruistic, they weren't. John refused to relinquish Thompson Street, which he had rented before our marriage and therefore, as he pointed out, it legally belonged to him. Since it seemed useless to argue, I moved into the West 10th Street sublet, thinking I had found peace at last.

I was wrong. One evening when I came home from a dinner date, there was my future ex-husband slumped in the living room's only armchair, drinking a martini. "How did you get in here?" I asked, dumbstruck.

"I think I'd better leave," my date nervously suggested.

"No, you stay. He'll leave."

"Like hell I will." John showed me a rip in his chinos. "I almost killed myself climbing over that fence out back." He gazed imperiously at my date. "I'm her husband, you know. And who might you be, pray tell?"

With a stricken look, the poor man bolted for the door and later said he never messed around with husbands whether they be present, future, or about to be ex. Neither did most men, I discovered. It seemed to be some kind of tacit masculine agreement that husbands were on sacred ground, no matter what they did or how outrageously they behaved.

"I've decided that I love you," John declared when we were alone.

"After four hellish years of marriage and countless infidelities, now you decide you love me?" I couldn't help laughing even though the joke was on me. "That's a riot."

"It's true, nonetheless."

"Well, I don't love you. You've come to your senses too late. You've hurt me too much. It's over."

"It can't be. I need you, Joyce."

"But I don't need you."

He measured me for a moment, then shrugged. "Okay, if that's how you want it, fine. I'm off."

"Goodbye."

"Goodbye forever, you rotten bitch."

Later that night while I was asleep, he sneaked back in over the fence and slept on the living room sofa keeping me awake with his thunderous snoring. The next morning we argued some more and he promised that if I didn't love him, he would let me alone.

"I don't love you," I said.

"Then you'll never lay eyes on me again."

A few nights later he was back, somehow managing to time his arrival with my return from dinner. Afterward I found out that he was following me and whomever I happened to be with. When my date had predictably fled, John launched into the betrayed husband routine again, overlooking the fact that it was I who had been faithful throughout our marriage, not he.

"Doesn't love mean anything to you?" was his standard opening line.

"It used to mean a lot before you started banging every woman with a heartbeat."

"Where did you hear that?"

"Only from all our friends. Even the men were shocked by your promiscuity. They said they never saw anyone exercise such little discretion or judgment. Apparently if a woman was warm, you screwed her."

"Why would I do that when I could have screwed you?"

Exactly what I had been trying to figure out. "You tell me."

"There's nothing to tell," he said, indignantly. "That's my point."

"Are you saying that all our friends are lying?"

"Of course they are. Now who are you going to believe? Those jerks or your own husband?"

There had been too much hard evidence against him. "Those jerks."

He got to his feet, albeit unsteadily. "In that case, I don't want to stay here. Goodbye forever, you miserable bitch."

The next time he climbed back in, he accused me of having no soul, no compassion and no brains. A few more weeks of his harassment and I was a wreck. Not only was he ruining my social life, but my sleep as well since passing out on the living room sofa had become a nightly habit of his, complete with the disruptive snoring. Something had to be done. I could either install iron bars on the windows, call the police and get a restraining order, or move. I didn't have enough money for the bars and for some reason I couldn't bring myself to call the cops, so I started looking around for new living quarters.

There were plenty of cheap apartments in New York in those days providing you could come up with two months' rent and a security deposit. Since I was only making sixty-three dollars a week before taxes as secretary to the Promotion Manager of the Simmons Company (Beautyrest mattresses and Hide-A-Bed sofas), I didn't have that kind of money. Nor did I have the obligatory deposit needed for Con Edison and AT&T. Considering my bleak financial situation and my legal rights, I should have gotten the restraining order and protected my little nest. Instead I panicked and ended up in the rooming house, my sole satisfaction being that my crazy husband would never get past the ever-vigilant Al.

"One day you'll look back at this and laugh," my friend Ted Peters said when he helped me move.

"Only derelicts and demented old ladies live in rooming houses. I'll bet there's a bottle of cheap gin in every room." By then I was sobbing. "I can't believe this is happening to me."

"It could be worse, kiddo. At least the place is clean," he said, looking around. "I might rent a room here myself."

Having recently been abandoned by his wife who ran off one night with their three-month-old son and was never heard from again, Ted repeatedly said that he couldn't go on living in their

Minetta Lane flat because of all the memories.

"What will I do about meals?" I asked as he put my two suitcases on the twin bed that was covered with a white chenille spread. "I can't afford to eat out."

That was when he offered me the rotisserie. "It's better than nothing and you can heat canned chili on it."

I had never eaten canned chili in my life. Another descent. I looked at the dark green window shades and bleak ray of light coming from the north and wondered if I would ever be happy again.

"What you need is a big steak and some red wine under your belt, so I'm taking you to Pete's for dinner." Ted, who worked as an editor at McGraw Hill, was a Hemingway aficionado and as convinced as his literary hero that the salutary effects of good food and drink would cure all ills. "I'll pick you up at seven. I'll bring the rotisserie."

In the months that followed, I came to look upon the rotisserie as a godsend. Even canned chili stopped depressing me. I found a way to mix it with corn niblets and Tabasco sauce and enjoy a hot meal in my little room. Other nights when I was alone, I ate dried apricots for dinner or bologna sandwiches with mayo and pickle relish. Ted took me out to dinner once a week before he moved into Irving Place Court and more often than that afterward, but meanwhile I was starting to meet new men.

The first new man I met was Wes Williams. He was a blind date arranged by my old pal Toni Kosover, who worked for *Seventeen Magazine* and would later become a fashion reporter for *Women's Wear Daily*. Toni was appalled by Irving Place Court. "It's even worse than your cold water flat on Thompson Street," she gasped. "How can you stand it?"

"It's not permanent." By then I had become quietly philosophical about my circumstances. "Besides, it will give me something to write about in years to come. I'm a starving artist. I toast corn muffins in a rotisserie. It's good material."

"Listen, I have a guy I want you to meet. He's rich, handsome, self-made and divorced. If you play your cards right, you can kiss this dump goodbye."

"What's he self-made at?"

"Wes owns a chain of dancing schools in the Midwest."

"Forget it."

"Oh, I see. He doesn't live in a garret and work as a grease monkey while spending weekends painting canvases that are going to set the world on fire. In other words, he's not like every loser you know. Is that it?"

"Close."

"Don't you want to improve yourself, Joyce? Be treated like a lady? Have someone take care of you?"

"You mean financially?"

"What else? Wouldn't you like to wear a mink coat in the winter instead of those cloth shmattes from Klein's? Wouldn't you like to spend Christmas in the Bahamas?"

I had never thought of men in those terms. "How old is this guy?"

"Thirty-nine."

I was twenty-five and very few of the men I knew were over thirty. "Isn't he kind of old for me?"

"When you see his apartment, you won't care about the fourteen-year age difference. Wes lives on Sutton Place, he has palm trees in his living room. And he wants to meet you. He's never met an aspiring writer before."

"I've never met a dancing school tycoon." I had an image of him soft-shoeing his way into the rooming house in top hat and tails, on the order of Fred Astaire, while he rhythmically struck his cane against my linoleum floor. "Okay, tell him to call me."

Toni glanced around. "I don't see a phone."

"It's down the hall. Tell him to let it ring, someone picks up sooner or later."

"I hope he's not turned off by this place," Toni said as she was leaving. "Wes is from Chicago."

"Don't they have rooming houses in the Windy City?"

"Not along Lake Michigan, you idiot. And please don't wear those bohemian black tights on your first date. This guy is class."

Wes Williams may have been a lot of things, but class wasn't one of them. He was a tall, dark, heavyset man whose tastes ran to sharkskin suits, pungent aftershave lotion and a pinky ring. He seemed impressed by me maybe because he sensed that I didn't want anything from him, unlike most of the women he'd known including his ex-wife.

"She was a two-bit gold digger and tried to bleed me white," he told me as we huddled in a choice banquette at the elegant Colony restaurant, sipping Taittinger brut. "If it weren't for our son, I wouldn't even be talking to the greedy broad. She's a barracuda. Not like you, sweet thing."

Having picked me up at the rooming house, he seemed just as horrified as Toni by my linoleum cell. An expression of sympathy filled his eyes and he asked if I knew any of my neighbors.

"Not a one." I didn't see the point in mentioning Ted who had recently moved into a ground-floor room and was letting me wash my hair in his shower. "Why do you ask?"

"I wondered what kind of people lived there."

"People like me who can't afford a real apartment, but I don't want your pity." In my best black wool dress and black suede spikes, I was feeling jaunty for the first time in weeks. "After I become a successful writer, Irving Place Court will seem like a dream."

He patted my hand. "Sure it will."

I didn't like his patronizing tone. "I'm serious, Wes."

"I know you are. What have you written?"

"A lot of short stories that were stolen in a trunk in Mexico."

"Were any of them published before they were stolen?"

"No. I've been rejected by every magazine in America, both the literary and commercial ones. I used to dread opening the mail for fear of finding another rejection slip."

"Doesn't that tell you something?"

"It tells me that short stories aren't my forte. I have to write a novel." I had gotten an idea for one that focused on what happened after my marriage broke up.

"What's stopping you?" Wes Williams wanted to know.

"Time. I have a nine-to-five job. I can't seem to dredge up the energy to write on weekends or at night. I'm too beat."

Wes slid his arm around my waist. "You need a husband, sweet thing."

"Wrong. I need a part-time job so I can write in the morning." John climbing over the back fence to get into my apartment would make a good scene.

"With a husband to support you, you would be able to write all day long." He flicked his tongue in my ear. "Just because you had one bad marriage doesn't mean the institution itself is at fault."

"That's debatable."

"I haven't let divorce make me bitter and you shouldn't either. The next time I tie the knot, it will be to a different kind of woman." He brushed his lips against my hair. "Someone like you, sweet thing."

When I refused to go to bed with him, he said he respected my wishes. "You want to get to know me better."

Actually I didn't and yet I continued to accept his dinner invitations because after a long day at the Simmons Company it was fun to dress up and drink imported champagne, be surrounded by attractive people, be pampered and catered to. Except for my weekly dinner date with Ted, the only time I ate a decent meal was when Wes Williams took me to one of Manhattan's top restaurants. Otherwise it was the usual dried apricots, bologna sandwiches and an occasional chili special. I had given the maid a few dollars not to tell Al about the rotisserie.

Since most of my meager paycheck went for clothes and the hairdresser rather than food, I lost some weight and suddenly became a perfect size five. Heavier women eyed me enviously and salesladies loved me because I fit into everything with no alterations needed. After a rushed lunch at Chock Full O' Nuts, I would head for B. Altman's Young Colony Shop to review their latest arrivals. The chemise, which had become popular that year, was made to order for my slip-hipped figure and if I'd had the money I would have bought out the entire store. I used to return to the office frustrated by my skimpy budget. One frustration led to another and before the day was over I was in despair about my inability to write, the lack of an apartment to call my own, and not least of all my personal life which seemed to be going nowhere.

As a result, I relented one night and let Wes Williams make love to me, thinking it might perk me up. It didn't. He was affectionate, inept, and as boring in bed as he was outside it. When I asked how he happened to go into the dancing school business, he said it was his ex-wife's idea. He wanted to open a chain of hardware stores, but the gold digger had no one to rhumba or mambo with and convinced him there was money to be made in giving lessons.

"I can't dance worth a damn," he admitted as he got out of bed (his bed) and put on a swirling silk robe that looked like the one Edward G. Robinson wore in *Key Largo* when he played a sleazy crime boss. Wrapping a blanket around myself, I followed Wes into the palm tree-studded living room where we sipped Jack Daniels on the rocks, listened to Andre Kostelanetz on the stereo and gazed at the East River glistening dimly off in the distance.

"Isn't this nicer than your rooming house?" he asked. "You can move in if you want to. You can use my son's bedroom as an office. He's only here on holidays. The gold digger managed to screw me out of extended visiting privileges, also."

"Thanks, Wes, but I don't think so."

"I meant until your divorce. Then we'll tie the knot."

"Even though I appreciate the offer, I have to make my own way in the world."

That tickled him. "Not when you have me, you don't. Think it over, sweet things. I'm in no rush."

I could redecorate, I mused, get rid of the palm trees, replace Hawaiian shmaltz with tasteful English chintz and a few antiques from Sotherby's, but when all was said and done what would I have? An English chintz apartment with a man who didn't read books and had never heard of Camus. No way, José.

"Who was that jerk in the Chesterfield overcoat I've seen you with lately?" Ted demanded one evening. His own sartorial tastes ran to a loden green duffle coat, popular with anti-establishment types. "He's been stopping by an awful lot."

"What are you, a private detective? The men I choose to go out with are my own business."

"I don't like his looks. Greasy, showy. I'll bet he wears a pinky ring."

It irritated me that he was right. "You mean you don't have a telephoto lens?"

"You can do better than a greaseball like that."

I had a hunch he meant I could do better with him. We had had a brief affair after both our marriages broke up, but it didn't amount to much. At least not to me. Now I suspected that Ted's feelings ran deeper and I wished they didn't. While I valued him as a friend, as a lover I found him possessive and overbearing.

"If I were you, I would be more selective in the future," he sternly advised me. "You can't go running around New York with every wisenheimer who asks."

"Why not? What else do I have to do in the evenings? Stare at the linoleum?"

"You could try writing."

He had hit a nerve. The more time that went by without writing, the more guilty and frightened I became. What if I never started my novel? I couldn't imagine a future that didn't include it and thanks to Ted's encouragement I began jotting down ideas for a plot, a theme, a time sequence, a cast of characters. Although it was gratifying, it wasn't the same as actually writing the book and the idea of having my mornings free to do just that seemed like the greatest luxury in the world.

"I've decided to get my marriage annulled," I told Ted not long afterward. We were in his room listening to Art Tatum and Bud Powell playing softly in the background. "I spoke to a lawyer and it's easier than I thought."

"Now you're making sense." He had been urging me to legally disentangle myself from John for as long as I could remember. "What made you see the light?"

"John began calling me at the office. Then a few days ago he showed up at the reception desk, dead drunk. It was a nightmare. He looked like he'd been rolling around in the gutter and he smelled like a brewery." I shuddered at the memory of the painful scene. "If he does it again, my boss said I'll probably get fired."

"Didn't you tell him that the two of you are separated and you're not responsible for his actions?"

"Sure, but Simmons is a very uptight conservative company. People who voted for Eisenhower aren't interested in their secretaries' personal problems. I was warned to keep John off the premises, or else."

"What did the creep want?"

"For me to go back to him. He was raving, begging, pleading, right there in Simmons' reception room with salesmen walking by and the V.P. in charge of advertising glaring at us. After I coaxed John downstairs, I told him that I was going to see a lawyer."

"What did he say?"

"Nothing. You know John. He never fights."

"Maybe if he did, he wouldn't drink so much," Ted shrewdly observed. "But why an annulment? Why not a divorce?"

"It's easier to get an annulment in New York State. You only have to prove fraud on the part of your mate. With divorce, you have to prove adultery which is more complicated—not to mention more expensive."

"What do you mean by 'fraud'?"

"I get up in court and swear that before we were married, John promised to buy a lovely home and let me decorate it to my heart's content. Then after we were married, he admitted he was broke and moved me into a crummy furnished room."

"It sounds simple enough. Is there anything I can do to help?"

"Would you be willing to serve him the subpoena? If he contests my actions, I can't proceed."

A lot of men might have been reluctant to become involved, but Ted looked as though I had just handed him the keys to a luxury yacht ready to cruise the Mediterranean at a moment's notice. "Would I be *willing?*" His laugh was gleeful. "I'd consider it a privilege."

The next day being Saturday, I had invited Ted and my old friend Harvey Anhalt up to my room for coffee and corn muffins. Harvey had moved into Irving Place Court a few weeks before and since he couldn't afford a private bathroom, I said he was free to soak in my tub on weekends. The communal john must have left a lot to be desired because he kissed my hand in gratitude. "Missy velly kind," he said, bowing and scraping.

When Harvey arrived he was wearing a handsome wool robe over tailored pajamas from Saks, one of the skimpy rooming house towels in his hand. He came from a well-off family who considered him a wastrel inasmuch as his only claim to fame was having typed the completed manuscript of *The Naked and the Dead*, Norman Mailer being his cousin by a previous marriage. Ted looked dashing in sharply pressed chinos and a blue Shetland sweater that matched his eyes while I was decked out in my latest purchase from the Young Colony Shop: a long at-home gown in red velours. Who would have guessed that among the three of us we didn't have a hundred dollars to call our own?

While Harvey bathed, Ted read the *Atlantic Monthly* and I gave myself a pedicure. Then over coffee we got around to discussing my upcoming annulment. Since Harvey was a close friend of John's, he found himself in an untenable situation when I asked if he would be willing to serve as my "Before" witness in court.

"I'd love to help you out, but John would kill me," he said with an apologetic smile. "John doesn't want to end your marriage. He's still in love with you."

Ted spoke up. "Does that mean the son of a bitch plans to contest the annulment? Because if so, I will personally break both his legs."

"I don't know what he plans to do," Harvey replied. "I only know that I hate to take sides. Why can't someone else be the 'Before' witness? What is that, anyway?"

"It's a mutual friend who claims he overheard John make the promise that he failed to keep," I explained. "I also need an 'After' witness who will testify that he heard John go back on his word once we were married."

I still couldn't believe my marriage had failed. I used to think that John and I would be together forever. He was my first love and I cared for him in a way that I suspected I would never care for another man as long as I lived.

"Maybe you can get Greta to be a witness," Harvey suggested. "She would probably be thrilled to get up on the stand, knowing that everyone was looking at her."

Greta Fletcher, a tall blonde who bore an uncanny resemblance to Kim Novak, was the love of Harvey's life. He had taken tantalizing photographs of her, which she planned to use to launch a modeling career after she whittled down her hips. Like her movie star lookalike, she was quite zaftig below the waist.

"The minute I have manageable hips, I'll be on the cover of every magazine in the country," she had declared. "It's only a question of time."

Harvey wasn't deterred by her hips or anything else for that matter. Not even the fact that their relationship was still in the platonic stage could dim his ardor. He told me there was nothing he wouldn't do in order to win Greta's heart including carrying her groceries, walking her toy poodle and picking up her laundry. She was gracious enough to indulge him on all counts.

My own friendship with Greta went back a few years to happier times. We used to sit in Washington Square park and fantasize about how we were going to be young mothers one day, just like the ones all around us who were watching their offspring play in the sunshine. But try as we did, neither of us managed to get pregnant. Then the painter with whom Greta had been living left her for another woman and my marriage broke up. At the age of twenty-five we found ourselves disillusioned with love and wondering why nature had conspired to keep us barren.

The next day it occurred to me that if I could convince Greta to testify on my behalf, I could probably persuade Harvey to do the same since he would be in her exalted company. At first Greta turned me down, saying she wasn't a morning person (we had to be at the Queens County Courthouse at some ungodly hour), but when I emphasized that she would be on the stand with a big group of onlookers hanging on her every word, she sullenly relented.

"What should I wear?" she asked, wetting her lips and staring at herself in a hand mirror that she carried in her purse. "How about my black dress with the sweetheart neckline? Too daring?"

"Much too daring." We had decided that she would be the "Before" witness and Harvey the "After." "I was thinking of your navy suit with a nice white blouse."

"Are you crazy? I can only wear white in the summer when I have a tan. Why do you think I stopped being a nurse? White is murder on my skin tone."

"Wear any color blouse you like just so long as it's not low-cut." She loved to show off her shoulders and cleavage in order to divert attention from her hips. "I want you to look dignified, ladylike."

"I can look dignified. Do you think a charge nurse runs around the hospital in a g-string and pasties?"

The morning of the hearing, saturnine Al stopped me as I was about to leave the rooming house. He wanted to know if Harvey was a junkie.

"Of course not," I snapped. "Where did you ever get such an absurd idea?"

"From the needle and syringe I found in his room."

"Don't you know that it's illegal to go through a tenant's personal possessions?"

"Heroin is what's illegal. If your friend is messing around with it, I'm throwing him out on his ass, *capish?*"

"Harvey happens to be diabetic. The only drug he's messing around with is insulin."

And Greta Fletcher, I felt like adding but there was no time for chit chat. Ted, Harvey and I had planned to meet Greta at the 23rd Street subway station so we could ride out to Queens together. She showed up looking glamorous in a fur-collared suede coat with a hot pink scarf draped around her neck. Harvey couldn't take his eyes off her.

"Guess what?" she whispered in my ear as the subway raced through the bowels of lower Manhattan. "I'm not wearing the navy suit."

Her coat was buttoned and tightly belted so I couldn't see what was underneath. "Don't do this to me, Greta. I'm nervous enough as it is."

"Navy is for the birds and, besides, I gave that suit to the Salvation Army." She smiled mischievously. "You have nothing to worry about, trust me."

What choice did I have? We were nearly there. Despite my apprehensions everything went according to plan, well, more or less. Greta had chosen to wear a high necked chocolate brown dress, with lipstick to match. She and Harvey answered my lawyer's carefully rehearsed questions with carefully rehearsed answers, both of them trying to look solemn and sincere while lying through their teeth.

"I was having dinner with Joyce and her future husband when I heard him promise to buy her a lovely home after they were married," Greta murmured in a soft but resonant voice, wetting her chocolate brown lips. "John said that since she had such good taste, she could decorate it any way she liked."

"In other words, he implied he had the money to pay for all that?" my lawyer prompted.

Greta paused dramatically and looked out at the sea of expectant faces, then at the cynical face of the judge. I could tell she was trying not to laugh and seated beside me, Harvey was trying to do the same. My friends were nothing if not irreverent when it came to the law.

"John certainly acted as if he had money. A lot of money," Greta said with a show of conviction. "If I were Joyce, I would have believed him."

Minutes later, Harvey was on the stand. "After they were married, John admitted that not only couldn't he afford to buy a house but he couldn't even come up with rent for a decent apartment."

Greta, who was back beside me, stifled a giggle while Ted wore an edgy smile. Even I felt moved to nervous laughter as I listened to Harvey's farcical testimony, wondering what the judge would think if he knew that John and I had spent the last few months of our marriage in sunny Acapulco.

"John said he would find the two of them a nice furnished room," Harvey droned on. "And if Joyce didn't like it, too bad."

"How did she react to this news?" my lawyer asked.

Harvey had been in Acapulco with us. "She burst out crying," he said gravely.

Afterward we celebrated with a festive Italian dinner at the San Remo, my lawyer having assured me that an annulment would be forthcoming.

"You realize what this means, don't you?" Ted said. "In the eyes of the law, you've never been married."

If only the law could obliterate my memories, I thought. The good ones, the bad ones, I wasn't free of any of them. I wasn't free of John either, not really. By shedding him, I had shed an essential part of myself that could never be recaptured and I missed him at that moment more than I would have ever thought possible.

Harvey's ex wife, Millie, was an accomplished actress who did a lot of work on radio soap operas. When she wasn't emoting on *Guiding Light* or *Helen Trent* she gave parties in her tiny mews house on East 26th Street. Although not far from Irving Place Court, it was light years away in charm.

Millie seemed to know all the interesting men in New York and managed to get them to come to her parties, which were lively affairs despite the limited space or maybe because of it. Strangers had a habit of finding themselves glued to other strangers on the narrow staircase and before long, they had become friends. In some cases, lovers. A lot of romances started in Millie's mews house, as did mine with Linton Cooper. Slight of build, wiry, sandy-haired and blue-eyed, Linton was from Pine Bluff, Arkansas. He had left his rural roots behind, he told me, in search of culture and erudition.

"Did you find them?" I asked.

"I surely did, Joyce." He spoke with a pronounced twang and was the only person who could make my first name sound as if it had two syllables. "In spades."

Describing himself as a journalist and linguist, he said he had been teaching school in the French Pyrenees but now that he was back in America he worked for a syndicated news service. My ears perked up. Linton seemed more like what the doctor ordered than dancing school Wes Williams, whom I had been avoiding lately.

"I've been trying to get hold of you," Wes grumbled when I finally answered the phone. "You're not cheating on me, are you, sweet thing?"

"Actually I've been busy getting my marriage annulled."

"Hey, this calls for a celebration. I'll reserve a table at '21' so wear your prettiest dress. We'll hit the Blue Angel afterward."

By then I was tired of wearing pretty dresses, ogling celebrities at the famed "21," tired of sitting in smoky nightclubs listening to sultry chanteuses sing the blues, then returning to palm tree heaven to make uninspired love. I was in the mood for a change and Linton Cooper was it. Unlike Wes, he didn't have much money. He wore casual Village-type clothes and wasn't appalled by my living in a rooming house or having a rotisserie in the bathroom. Considering his general attitude, I couldn't help thinking that Ted would approve of him.

"Who's that jerk in the blue windbreaker I've seen you running around with lately?" Ted asked, having called me at the office one afternoon. "He looks like big trouble to me."

"For your information, he happens to be a freelance journalist and a very nice guy. Very unassuming."

"I don't trust a grown man who wears mittens. Where does this jerk live?"

"In a cold water flat on Carmine Street. It reminds me of the one that John and I had on Thompson Street, except Linton's bathtub isn't in the kitchen. It's in the hallway between the living room and the bedroom." The peculiarity of the location hadn't escaped me.

"His bathtub could be in the middle of Central Park for all I care. What bothers me is that this jerk has no regard for your safety."

"How did you arrive at that conclusion?"

"He lets you go home alone and not by taxi either. I've seen you trudging down the street from the bus stop late at night. At least Chesterfield Overcoat had the decency to put you in a cab even if he didn't come along for the ride. I worry about you, kiddo. You have the worst taste in men I've ever run across."

"I see that you bought the telephoto lens after all. What do you do, Ted? Sit by your window and watch my comings and goings?"

"Somebody has to. I thought that when you left John, I could relax my vigil but lately I've started to realize that the trouble has only just begun."

"You're weird, Ted. Do you know that?"

"*I'm* weird? I'm not the one taking baths in a tub that might as well be sitting on the sidewalk for all the privacy it affords you. I'll bet that guy hasn't bothered to put up a shower curtain, has he?"

It galled me that he was right.

"He's probably a slob, too."

"Well, he isn't." While Linton's apartment was on the messy side, he himself was immaculate and had a habit of suddenly ripping off his clothes and running a fast tub. "Cleanliness is next to godliness," he was fond of saying in that twangy voice of his. Still he did have some strange habits that I thought best not to reveal to Ted. The way he heated his cold water flat, for instance. Most people installed a pot bellied stove as John and I had done, but not Linton. Maybe he couldn't afford one or maybe he was a stoic. He relied on his fireplace, but it didn't keep the apartment warm enough. Even though I always wore several layers of clothing when I went to visit, my teeth chattered and my feet felt like ice. The only thing that helped was a shot of Jack Daniels, which happened to be Linton's favorite alcoholic beverage just as it was Wes's. It amused me because otherwise the two men had nothing in common. Well, except for me, of course.

Linton liked to cook and, being Southern, his specialties ran to black-eyed peas, collard greens, deep-fried chicken, buttermilk biscuits and mashed potatoes with country gravy. I found it pretty indigestible fare after the spartan diet I had been on, but diligently cleaned my plate and complimented the chef. Afterward we would listen to Vivaldi or Mozart and then make love on his built-in bed that didn't have a box spring.

To my disappointment, Linton was no more accomplished a lover than Wes Williams and a lot less affectionate to boot, which squelched any ideas I might have had of getting serious and I relegated him to the "temporary affair" category. That I now had two men in the same category presented no problem as I began dividing my time between them. When I got bored with one, I went to see the other. Since they moved in such different circles, it seemed highly unlikely they would ever meet or compare notes.

Only Ted was aware of my double life. "Two-timer," he said to me, but not without a flicker of admiration.

"I'm glad you approve, for a change."

"Who approves? I think you're playing with fire."

"Not if I don't get burned."

Over the next few months I was off and running. With brief stops at Irving Place Court for refueling, I ran uptown, downtown, Eastside, Westside, all around the town, determined to distract myself, enjoy myself at all costs, my own pleasure being my main priority. Love held no appeal for me any longer, I couldn't afford the vulnerability. I couldn't be hurt again, not to soon after the dissolution of my marriage. (Sometimes I woke up in the middle of the night and reached out for John.) I hardened myself to feelings and concentrated on façades. Objects. Surfaces. On how things looked. Like the buildings that Wes and Linton lived in.

The contrast couldn't have been greater. Wes's was a tall white tower on exclusive Sutton Place with a uniformed doorman opening the portals to a lobby of travertine floors and Persian runners, oil paintings on the walls and a red velvet bench on which to sit while waiting for the manned elevator. Linton's building was a decayed tenement on an old Italian street in the Village with a broken front door, bicycles and baby carriages cluttering the shabby vestibule, no elevator and a winding metal staircase that was hell on high heels and reeked of garlic.

"Doesn't it make you feel a little schizoid to date two such different men at the same time?" Millie asked me, her eyes hot with curiosity after I had whimsically decided to tell her about my new lifestyle. "Don't you feel guilty for cheating on one with the other?"

"After all the cheating John did on me?"

"What does John have to do with it?"

"Nothing." Meaning everything. "I never promised Wes or Linton that I would be faithful and they didn't make any promises either."

"Which one do you prefer?"

"When I'm with Wes, I prefer Linton. And vice versa. I guess it means I could live quite happily without either one, but at the moment they're a diversion."

"From what?"

"Everything I don't want to think about. The annulment. The inability to write. The lack of money. The rooming house." The longer I stayed at Irving Place Court, the more fervently I yearned for a real nest of my own. "The list is endless."

"You said that Wes wants to marry you. Wouldn't that solve all your problems?"

It wouldn't solve not being married to John. "I can't marry Wes. One evening with him and I'm climbing the walls. Why do you think I go running down to the Village the next night to see Linton? At least I can talk to him about books and writing. He's read all the classics."

"Then maybe it's Linton you should marry, or live with. It sounds as though the two of you have a lot in common."

"Only superficially. After we're through exchanging literary opinions, there's nothing left to say. Wes may not have heard of Camus, but he has a feel for people that Linton lacks."

"If I were you, I would opt for Wes and make the best of it," Millie said. "Be realistic, Joyce. You can't have a gorgeous apartment on Sutton Place, free time to write, no money worries and an intellectual giant too."

"Why not? It's what I feel I deserve."

A few weeks later, Linton introduced me to the man who would become my literary agent. Linton didn't know Sterling Lord, but he knew Sterling's second wife, Danielle, from the time he lived in France. "She's invited us to dinner next week," he told me. "Danielle is quite the Parisienne. You'll like her."

I was more interested in touching base with Sterling who had begun to make a name for himself in the publishing world. That he and his new wife were madly in love seemed apparent as soon as we walked in the door of their Upper East Side apartment. Danielle was dark haired, lovely, sophisticated. Sterling was fair haired, broad shouldered, masculine. They couldn't keep their eyes off each other and although both were unfailingly polite, I had the impression that they wouldn't be too unhappy when we left. Danielle cooked a simple meal—a ham omelet and tossed salad—but what made it so special was the glow that pervaded the room. I felt envious of my hosts and wondered if I would ever again be as deeply in love.

During dinner I reminded Sterling that we had met briefly some years before. A mutual acquaintance, Mickey Nathanson (who would later write *The Dirty Dozen*) had suggested that I send my short stories to Sterling in hopes of getting him to represent me.

"You turned me down flat," I now told him. "You said you weren't taking on any new clients. I was devastated."

"Perhaps we can rectify that," he agreeably replied. "What are you writing at the moment?"

"I'm just about to start my first novel. Can I send it to you when it's finished?"

"Even before if you'd like. I'd be glad to give you my opinion."

Suddenly I felt more optimistic than I had in months. Maybe a sign of professional encouragement was what I had needed all along to start saving money for an apartment, trade in my full-time job for a part-time one, and begin my book. By now I had a complete plot outline as well as a folder crammed with notes. I could see my characters in action, hear them talking, they had become very real to me and I couldn't wait to spend chunks of uninterrupted time with them.

I got up early the next day and devised a new budget for myself. If I saved twelve dollars a week for three months, I would have enough money to put down on a cheap apartment and with severance pay from Simmons I could make it livable. Saving twelve dollars a week from a paycheck of sixty-three dollars before taxes wasn't easy, but because I felt so motivated I cut my expenses to the bone. No more shopping excursions at the Young Colony Shop and no more lunches at Chock Full O' Nuts, however cheap they were. I started to brown bag it. I even stopped going to the hairdresser for a

monthly trim and let my
except the most essential

Sometime during th
proposed to me. He had j
after the opening of a sm
in a place like this," he sa
doing here to start with, b
of your system. Okay, its

"Wes, I don't think—"

"Let me finish. With
ready for a more mature
think you know what I'm

"Yes, and I wish you w

"Will you marry me,
happy. I'm moving into a
has a wraparound terrace a
for us, one for my son whe
own studio to write in. Wh

I said it was a very ge
explained my own moving

"I don't get it." He wa
one dump for another. W
could be married to me an

"I don't love you, Wes."

"In time, that will chan

"You're wrong. If I do
resent you for interfering

"Those are some plans

"They may not sound l
to me. I've put this book o
write it."

He was getting angry. "
won't have any marital resp

"That's right. I don't ha

First Novel: 1956

IT'S A GOOD THING we can't see ahead because had I known that *Getting Rid of Richard* wouldn't be published for sixteen years, I would probably have lost my nerve and never started it. Actually "nerve" is one of the qualities it takes to tackle a first novel, the others being an inflated ego and a gambler's crazed sense of bravado, all of which I felt imbued with, more or less, when I sat down to write my account of one woman's efforts to keep her ex-husband, a deranged fence jumper, out of her apartment and life.

If the plot was semi-autobiographical, the one-week time frame in which the story unfolded was pure fiction. To show what my heroine's marriage had been like and why it broke up, I planned to use a series of vivid flashbacks in addition to the current action, hoping that four hundred pages would cover it. I still remember typing the title page on my manual Smith-Corona with clammy hands and a racing heart. When I came to the words, "A novel by Joyce Elbert," I heard the New York Philharmonic break into Wagnerian praise for a major new literary voice, yet seconds later doubt and insecurity had crept in.

This unnerving seesaw of emotions would continue on and off throughout the course of the book. One day I would feel convinced I was a genius, the next day I would feel like a fraud. What helped give me confidence was the desk in my new Bank Street studio apartment, the landlord having said it was installed by previous tenant, John Howard Lawson, one of the famous Hollywood ten dissenters.

"John Howard Lawson?" I said, dumbfounded. "Are you sure?"

"Of course I'm sure. Why?" He didn't understand my reaction, never having heard of John Howard Lawson. "Don't you like it?"

"I love it!"

The desk had been cleverly built into a wall between two windows and painted flat back, a popular color in the Village in those days since it hid all dirt and imperfections. A running joke about furniture was that no matter how decrepit its condition, all you had to do to make it serviceable was cut off the legs and paint it flat black. As far as I was concerned the desk could have been painted cherry red, my admiration for the Hollywood Ten being boundless. At the time I didn't know that John Howard Lawson was a fervent Communist with no sense of humor.

I only knew that he had authored a brilliant tome called *The Theory and Technique of Playwriting* and become a folk hero during one of the most ignominious periods in American history. This meant that one day I would be able to say I had written my first novel on a desk belonging to a man who went to prison rather than betray his colleagues to a witch-hunting Senate Investigating Committee. To my mind, that statement would look pretty impressive on the back of the dust jacket of *Getting Rid of Richard*, beneath a photo of the attractive young author wearing a sultry smile and a pair of diamond drop earrings. Yes, indeedy.

To write novels had been my goal ever since I was seventeen and I switched majors literally overnight, going from French to Journalism. I chose Journalism rather than English because it allowed me to take a wider variety of writing classes, not because I had any intention of becoming a reporter. *What* happened was rarely as interesting to me as *why* it happened and now after nine years of postponing my heart's desire, I was about to make it a reality. While I had no reason to assume I could succeed where so many had failed, I did assume it. I had to in order to confront the enormous task that lay ahead.

I nervously put a sheet of paper into the typewriter, thinking this was it. The day of reckoning. Ready, set, go. Then I stopped cold, unable to remember the names of any of my characters, my mind a total and utter blank. Had this ever happened to Jane Austen or

Virginia Woolf? After checking my notes, I typed their names on a piece of paper and taped it to John Howard Lawson's flat black desk.

One month after I started *Getting Rid of Richard*, I realized that my money was running out and I had to get a part-time job. Since it made no sense to look uptown due to the precious time I would lose in transportation, I considered the employment possibilities within walking distance of where I lived. Two came to mind: New York University and Fairchild Publications. I flipped a coin. Heads NYU, tails Fairchild. It came up tails. The next day wearing one of my two summer skirts and a freshly ironed blouse, I set off for 7 East 12th Street and timed my walk for future reference. Twelve minutes.

"I'll do anything," I told Wight Martindale, the Personnel Manager, a pleasant looking middle-aged man, who regarded me impassively. "I can type, take shorthand, file, answer the phone, work a switchboard, be a copygirl, sweep the floor. I want to work from one to five and clear fifty dollars a week. Do you have a job for me?"

"How fast is your shorthand?"

"A hundred words a minute. I realize that's not super fast, but someone had borrowed the Gregg book from the library so I had to settle for Pitman. While it's slower, it's more accurate," I assured him.

"Are you saying you taught yourself shorthand from a library book?" (Years later he admitted that he thought I was a nut case.)

"That's right, Mr. Martindale. I couldn't afford to go to shorthand school."

"My secretary is on vacation at the moment. Maybe you can fill in for her."

I couldn't believe my good luck. "When do I start?"

He smiled. "Sit down, Miss Elbert. I have a lot of correspondence."

Even though my shorthand wasn't as fast as I pretended, I have a good memory and a feel for the way people talk. Also I was a fast typist and an utterly compulsive worker. It never occurred to me to take a break, get a cup of coffee or go to the ladies room. I just sat there and typed. An hour later, Wight Martindale was astonished when I handed him the letters for his signature. "You can do what you said you could do, Miss Elbert." He was looking at me with new eyes. "And very quickly at that."

"Does that mean I have a job?"

"A temporary job if you want it. You can work for me until my secretary returns and then since it's summer and a lot of the girls are on vacation, you can pinch-hit in some of the other departments. Providing you don't mind moving around from time to time."

"I don't mind at all."

"I'll tell Accounting that you're an independent contractor, which means they won't deduct taxes from your paycheck. That will be your responsibility."

I loved the idea of being an independent contractor.

"One more thing," Wight Martindale said. "If you want to clear fifty dollars a week, you'll have to work from one to six."

I would still have my mornings free. "It's a deal," I said, shaking his hand.

My days quickly fell into an agreeable routine. In the morning I wrote, stopping at noon to shower, dress, grab a sandwich and set out on the twelve-minute walk to Fairchild Publications. From one to six, I took dictation and typed letters, memos, reports, whatever needed typing. After work I went home, prepared a solitary dinner and wrote some more, although some evenings I broke this routine to go out with my current boyfriend, German-born painter Friedl Dzubas. I had met Friedl in Easthampton the previous summer, not long after Jackson Pollack was killed in that famous car accident. Friedl, who had been sharing a house with him and art critic Clem Greenburg, said that if it weren't a car accident it would have been some other fatality. "Vhen you are as self-destructive as Jackson Pollack iss not goot."

While I liked Friedl's wacky accent and disarming smile, I wasn't ready for a committed relationship. Friedl, on the other hand, had been divorced for quite some time and was anxious to settle down. "Vhy you don't vant to get serious?" he kept asking. "Vhat's wrong viss me?"

I was too polite to admit that aside from our bad timing, I couldn't stand the way he painted. An abstract expressionist, I found his colors mawkish and sentimental. One day during an argument he accused me of being cynical and I accused him of having a pastel soul.

"In zhat case, Chagall has pastel soul, too," he shot back.

"I couldn't agree more."

"You don't like Chagall?" He was incredulous. "Tell me who are your favorite painters."

"De Chirico, Munch and Hopper." I purposely left out Matisse just to make him crazy.

Friedl was incensed. "Vhat a threesome! Vhat a depressing voman you are! Vhat am I going to do viss you?"

"Do you want to break up?"

"No, I vant to know vhy you only like dark painters."

"Hopper isn't dark."

"Iss grim, iss same thing. Vhy you don't like a cheerful man like Chagall?"

"I hate those people of his dancing in mid-air."

He looked at me accusingly. "You vouldn't also happen to like Magritte and Grant Vood, vould you?"

"How'd you guess, Friedl?"

After a rocky start, *Getting Rid of Richard* was picking up steam and when I hit page fifty I felt as though a milestone had been reached, while at the same time I felt increasingly anxious about the number of pages still to come. Then I realized that if I were to persevere, I had to stop dwelling on the road ahead and concentrate on the here and now. With that in mind, I resolved to write a minimum of three pages a day from then on and not think beyond those pages. If I did that faithfully six days a week, at the end of six months I would have a completed manuscript. Although it was hard to believe, I told myself that numbers don't lie.

I tried to end each day's stint while I was still going strong, so that when I sat down again I wouldn't be stumped for openers. Sometimes I even quit in mid-sentence, a little gimmick I borrowed from Papa Hemingway, and it helped stifle my fear of drying up. The further into my book I went, the more obsessed with it I became and pretty soon I was breaking dates with Friedl or not making them at all. He resented my priorities and told me that if I continued like this, I would end up a lonely old woman.

Even though I brushed off his dire prediction, it took its toll. The evenings that I stayed home and wrote, I wondered if I should have gone out with Friedl but when I did, I wished I had stayed home and wrote. Trying to achieve a happy balance between my personal and professional life wasn't easy since in those days women weren't supposed to be focused on a career, but on their husbands, boyfriends, or fiancés. To a certain extent, they still are.

"I haf never seen anything like it," my gynecologist said in an accent that was uncannily similar to Friedl's. "Something very peculiar iss going on viss you."

I had gone to see Dr. Elsa LaRoe when I skipped my period and was feeling nauseated. My heroine in *Getting Rid of Richard* thought she was pregnant and even though I always used a diaphragm, I wondered if this was a case of life copying art. After examining me, Dr. LaRoe took a rabbit test which to my relief came out negative. No way was I about to bear Friedl's child, yet the prospect of an illegal abortion was just as scary. Dr. LaRoe said I was very anemic and put me on a regimen of B-12 and liver shots, but to her astonishment they failed to work and my blood count remained ominously low.

"Those injections always vork," she said, puzzled.

She took another rabbit test and the result turned out negative again, leading her to conclude that anemia was preventing me from menstruating as my body couldn't spare the blood. Meanwhile I was becoming more weak and nauseated with every passing day. Some mornings I could barely drag myself out of bed. Friedl wasn't much help.

"One of these days the rabbit vill die and then ve vill get married."

"No, we won't because I'm not pregnant."

By then I almost wished I were since it would explain why I was so bloated that I couldn't button my skirt, even though I hadn't gained an ounce. Dr. LaRoe was mentally tearing her hair out, trying to diagnose the problem. She was a tough feisty woman married (for the third time) to a hat designer half her age. Born in Germany, she had entered medical school at a time when women weren't encouraged to work, let alone become doctors. She started the first birth control clinic in Heidelberg and said she had divorced her Nazi husband when he moved into the higher echelons of Hitler's inner circle.

Dr. LaRoe despised Hitler and everything he stood for. According to her, the Führer was sexually arrested. "He used to haf an orgasm vhenever he stood on that balcony and vatched his followers stick out their arms and shout, 'Heil Hitler.' Yes, then he vould ejaculate, the dirty little man."

"What about Eva Braun?"

"She vas like his daughter, not his sveetheart." Dr. LaRoe made a face of disgust. "Hitler was afraid of real vomen, they frightened him. Vatch out for vegetarians, iss all I vill tell you."

Not long afterward the reason for my condition turned up in the toilet bowl. I couldn't believe my eyes. At the risk of sounding totally gross, I saw a long dark squirmy thing just before I flushed. Fortunately I had the presence of mind to scoop it out and put it in a jar. Seconds later all of my symptoms had disappeared and I felt like my old healthy self again. I tried to call Dr. LaRoe, but her line was busy and I called Friedl.

"Gott im Himmel!" he cried. "You haf vorms."

"I have what?"

"Vorms! Vorms!" Then he lapsed into a torrent of German.

I felt sure I had misunderstood. "Are you saying I have worms?

How is that possible? I thought only dogs got worms. Or do you mean a tapeworm?"

"For that, you vill haf to consult your doctor." He chuckled. "Vorms! Who vould haf thought of such a thing?"

When I tried Dr. LaRoe again, her response was identical to Friedl's. "Gott im Himmel!" she cried. "You haf vorms!"

"So I gather."

"Bring in the specimen immediately and ve vill haf it analyzed. Then ve vill know vhat kind of vorms ve are dealing viss."

"What do you mean 'dealing with'? It's all over. I feel fantastic."

"Iss not over, Joyce, iss only beginning." She made a clucking sound. "Vorms! Vhy didn't I suspect?"

"Only beginning? Are you telling me there's more than one?"

"Hundreds."

I have only fainted once in my life and this wasn't it, but I came close. The idea that I might be harboring hundreds of those long dark squirmy things in my intestines made my head spin. "I'll be right over," I croaked.

The cure was almost worse than the disease and I don't know how I made it through the next two months. It seems that intestinal parasites breed at an alarming rate and the purpose of the prescribed antibiotics was not only to destroy those that already existed, but also every egg they laid. To make sure this was accomplished, periodic tests were mandatory and I began shlepping to a lab on the Upper East Side after work, carrying a turd in a mayonnaise jar.

On one such occasion I was wearing a beautiful silk dress and a black velvet cape because Friedl was taking me to a party at the swank River Club that evening. I wondered what would happen if I were hit by a truck and when the police opened my purse looking for identification, they found the jar with the shit. Although this kind of dark humor gave me a chuckle, it didn't last long since I had never felt so desolate or unclean in my life. Eventually I lost all interest in sex as well any desire for human companionship. All I wanted to do was crawl into a corner and die. Friedl couldn't understand why I was avoiding him.

"I luf you," he said.

"I'm too sick to deal with love."

He noticed the sheet of paper in my typewriter. "But not too sick to vork, I see."

"Writing is the only thing that has kept me from blowing my brains out during this entire ghastly period."

"Zhanks a lot," he said.

It was around this time that my fortunes at Fairchild Publications took an interesting turn. For months I had dutifully trudged off to whichever of their six trade newspapers I was sent. I did whatever was asked of me. I never complained or requested a transfer. No lowly task was beneath me until I spent an afternoon in the advertising department of *Women's Wear*, filing three-by-five index cards. During my break, I ran up to Personnel and threw myself upon the mercy of Wight Martindale's secretary.

"You've got to get me out of there," I told Mary Vogel. "I can't take another week of filing index cards or I'll go crazy, not to mention blind."

"I'm afraid I don't have another regular opening at the moment, but Wade Fairchild's secretary is out sick today. If you want, you can fill in for her. However it will only be for a day or two."

Although there were several Fairchilds floating around the premises, I had never heard of one called Wade. "He's Louis's and Edgar's nephew," Mary explained, referring to the president and vice president of the company. "Mr. Wade is starting a new publication called *Electronic News*."

He could have been starting a porno magazine for all the difference it made to me. I found his office inauspiciously located not far from the fourth floor ladies' room and went barging in. He was in the middle of a sales meeting. "Are you Wade Fairchild?" I asked, coming face to face with a tall, lanky, prematurely white-haired young man. "Because if you are, I'm begging you to save my life."

"Who are you?" he asked with an amused smile.

"Joyce Elbert and I understand your secretary is out sick." There was her deserted desk with a cover over the typewriter. It looked like heaven to me. "Let me work for you, please!"

"Sure, but try to calm down." After he ended the meeting, he handed me a list of names. "These are the men who will be selling advertising space for *Electronic News* in the future. We met recently in Chicago and I want to send each of them a thank-you note, but I don't want the notes to be identical. Do you think you could word them slightly differently, as a personal touch?"

"Boy, are you ever talking to the right person," I said, taking the cover off his secretary's typewriter.

When Wade's secretary returned a few days later, he offered me a permanent part-time job working for two of his space salesmen and I gratefully accepted. Although neither of us could have known it then, our professional relationship would stretch over the next ten years with time out for me to get married, move to Paris, get divorced, move to Mexico, etc. Our friendship lasted until his recent death.

"How come you only work part-time?" Wade asked me after I had been there awhile. "Do you have an ailing mother at home?"

Until then I hadn't told anyone how I spent my mornings, but somehow I didn't mind telling Wade that I was writing a novel. His face lit up and he admitted that when he was an undergraduate at Princeton he had dreams of following in the footsteps of its most famous literary alumnus, F. Scott Fitzgerald. "I got suckered into the family business instead," he said, wryly. "I give you credit for doing what you want, it takes guts. But why haven't you asked Personnel to transfer you to one of our editorial departments? Wouldn't you rather be a reporter?"

"No because I would have to work full-time."

"When do you think you'll finish the book?"

"Hopefully by the spring."

"What happens then?"

"I get an agent and let him take it from there." I wondered if Sterling Lord would still want to represent me after he read *Getting Rid of Richard*. "However that's for when the war is over. Right now I'm in the trenches."

I had come to realize that writing a novel was a battle. Even though it took talent, imagination and an inflated ego, none of those qualities would save the day unless the writer was willing to go to the front lines and fight for her book. My enemies were apathy, loss of confidence, laziness and fear of failure. There were mornings when I didn't feel like fighting, when I felt like sleeping late or dawdling over coffee, but I went to the typewriter and fought. Sometimes not much came of it. Sometimes I tore up more pages than I saved. Sometimes I couldn't produce three pages no matter how hard I tried. Sometimes I was convinced the battle wasn't worth winning, that *Getting Rid of Richard* had no merit. Sometimes I thought I was crazy to try writing a novel at all. Sometimes I considered burning the manuscript and looking for another line of work.

But I was too stubborn to admit defeat and there were rewards, often unexpected ones. Just when I was on the verge of giving up on a difficult scene, a new approach would present itself. A plot change that I hadn't considered would flash across my mind and solve several problems all at once. Dialogue that had sounded flat and lifeless would miraculously take on a new sparkle thanks to a turnabout in one of the character's attitudes. Breakthroughs like that made the dark days bearable and gave me hope. And so I pushed on, convinced I would win the war yet.

My worm cure finally complete, I started going out again, mostly to parties on weekends. It was December in New York and everyone seemed to be throwing a party. Each Saturday night I managed to meet a handsome stranger who would invite me to another party the following Saturday. After Friedl's intensity, I liked gallivanting around town with a slew of different men who were no more enamored of me than I was of them. One weekend Romeo stands out.

Harry was a tall husky Ivy League type who shaved on the subway. We were on the "A" train going to a bash on Central Park West when he took out a can of shaving cream and began lathering up. He had brought along a hand mirror so he could see what he was doing and not cut himself. Within seconds, he had the undivided attention of everyone in the car.

"People go ape when they see me doing this," he confided, scraping shaving cream off his chin, looking very pleased with himself. "Am I embarrassing you?"

"Why should I be embarrassed? I'm not the one who's acting like a jerk."

"Most girls think it's kind of cute."

"'Cute' is my least favorite word in the English language."

"I love you, too," Harry said.

As soon as we walked into the party, which was being held in one of those fortress-like pre-war buildings, he disappeared into the crowd. I was standing in a corner nursing a weak gin and tonic when a curly-haired blond man sauntered over. He had heavily-fringed blue eyes and a dazzling smile. "You look lonely," he said.

"My date just dumped me."

"What's wrong with him?"

"He shaves in the subway."

"No, I'm serious."

"So am I."

Within minutes, we were smitten. His name was Tom King and he did something in production at ABC Television. He had come to the party with a married couple whom he introduced to me. Mary and Alan Abrons lived in Hastings-on-the-Hudson and seemed very suburban, affluent. I later learned that Alan's father was a well known real estate developer with extensive holdings in Manhattan. When they saw how Tom was looking at me, they invited me to their home for Sunday brunch.

"I'd love to come," I said. "Which Sunday?"

"How about tomorrow?" Alan replied. "In fact why don't you

drive back with us tonight and sleep over?"

It was such an offbeat suggestion that I accepted on the spot. The Abrons' home was a lovely rambling Tudor with lots of Louis XV furniture and original paintings. Alan took Tom and me upstairs, then asked if I wanted my own bedroom. "Of course, I do." I was startled. "What did you think?"

"He lives vicariously through me," Tom said, laughing.

I was beginning to regret my impetuousness. I didn't know these people. They could be mass murderers, sexual deviants. They could hold me captive and nobody would ever find me. Since there was no lock on my door I felt too anxious to fall asleep, although toward morning I finally drifted off into a restless slumber when I thought I heard someone enter the room. I opened my eyes. No one was there. Had I been dreaming? It was a relief to get dressed, albeit in last night's party clothes, and go downstairs for coffee.

"Did you sleep well?" Alan asked, a sly smile on his face. Mary was buried in the Sunday papers.

"Not very. I dreamed that someone came into my room. At least I think it was a dream."

"My husband sleepwalks," Mary said, without looking up. "But he's harmless."

"Absolutely harmless," Alan agreed.

"Then it *was* you?"

"Sleepwalkers can't remember where they've been. One night I walked three miles to town and had no recollection of it the next day."

When Tom and I boarded the train to return to the city, I said I never wanted to visit the Abrons again. "There's something creepy about the two of them. I don't believe that sleepwalking story of his for a second. I think Mary was covering for him. I think he's a peeping Tom, pardon the pun."

"You're not far wrong. Alan was pretty sure he would find the two of us together. That's how he gets his kicks, poor man."

"Sick man, you mean."

"Mary has cut him off and he's hurting. He's not really a bad sort."

"Debatable," I said, wondering why Tom was defending him.

Tom and I knew many of the same people, we soon discovered, making it extremely likely that our paths had crossed before. He told me that he started out to be an actor on the Broadway stage just around the time my ex-husband started out to be a playwright. It was fun to compare notes on mutual acquaintances and return to favorite haunts in the theatre district, but the fun began to fade when I realized how absurdly possessive he was. If another man so much as glanced at me, Tom became furious although he managed to control himself until we were alone. Then the full extent of his jealousy came pouring out.

"You encouraged that guy!" he cried one night. "I saw you looking over your shoulder, leading him on. Who is he, anyway? Did you have an affair with him? Were you in love with him?"

"I don't even know who you're talking about," I truthfully replied.

"I'll bet you don't." His face was contorted with anger, suspicion. "Maybe you're still in love with him. Is that what's going on?"

"Nothing is going on. You have to believe me."

"How can I when you're always flirting with an ex-boyfriend behind my back? Don't you know what that does to me? I'm crazy about you. I can't bear to think of you with another man."

"But we've both been with other people in the past." Tom had been married twice. "That's my point: they're in the past. Now we're with each other."

"So you admit you used to be involved with that guy," he triumphantly declared. "At last the truth comes out!"

No matter what I said, I couldn't win and before long I fell into the insidious trap of playing by Tom's rules, which meant trying to keep his suspicions in abeyance, trying to soothe the savage beast. Today a great deal is known about the dangers of becoming involved with overly possessive men, but in 1956 that kind of behavior was considered a sign of caring and love. Syndromes such as date rape, sexual harassment and domestic violence were not only still to be coined, the police and judicial systems invariably took the man's side, convinced that the woman in question had been "asking" for it, whatever "it" happened to be.

To keep Tom happy, I prayed that no man would look my way and gradually I began to wear less makeup and dress less provocatively in hopes of avoiding masculine attention. Then one evening at a party I made the mistake of dancing briefly with the host and didn't hear the end of it for hours afterward. "That guy is infatuated with you," Tom ranted. "What was he whispering in your ear? Did he ask you to get rid of me and meet him later on? Were the two of you lovers before he was married?"

"We were never lovers and he wasn't whispering in my ear. He was singing along with the music."

"In your ear," Tom insisted, his voice rife with fury.

"Where should he have been singing? In my nose?"

Instead of getting a laugh out of him, all I got was dead silence for the next twenty-four hours and yet I still didn't realize how sick he was. Later I would wonder why not and could only conclude that nothing in my life had prepared me for pathological jealousy or where it might lead. Nothing had ever taught me to be afraid. A few days later I was coming home from the supermarket, loaded down with groceries, when I heard a familiar voice. "Dr. Livingstone, I presume?"

I whirled around and there on the sidewalk was my ex-husband, whom I hadn't laid eyes on in over a year. "I'm surprised to see you," I said. "I thought you were living in Provincetown."

"I am." John relieved me of several packages. "I'm just passing through."

I invited him up to my apartment for coffee and once inside, wished I hadn't. It was too painful being reminded of the years we had spent together, the dismal breakup, the lingering regrets, the love that had never completely died in spite of everything. It was a chillingly cold day. We made a fire and we made small talk, but I was glad when he finally left. Later that evening Tom and I stopped for a drink at a bar on West 45th Street before going to the theatre. Since the bar happened to be one that John and I used to frequent during the early days of our marriage, I wasn't surprised to see him having a drink with an attractive redhead. He spotted me at the same time and waved.

"Who's that?" Tom wanted to know.

"My ex-husband. I ran into him this morning when I was coming back from the supermarket."

Tom didn't say another word and I naïvely thought it was because he understood how innocent our encounter had been. We finished our drinks and went to see *The Chalk Garden*. Although I found it strange that he continued to be so quiet, I never connected it to my ex-husband. Tom remained silent in the taxi going home, but the minute we walked into my apartment he punched me clear across the room. I was too stunned to believe it had happened. I guess I was in shock. No man had ever hit me before. Masculine violence was not only unknown to me, it was unthinkable, unfathomable. If he had been a stranger, I might have tried to protect myself, but he was my boyfriend, my lover. "Are you crazy?" I cried. "Are you totally out of your mind?"

"You're the one who's crazy if you think you can two-time me with your ex-husband and get away with it, you unfaithful bitch."

"No one's been two-timing you. Where do you get these absurd ideas?"

"I'll show you who's absurd, you whore."

His fist smashed into my face. Then he proceeded to beat me up and I am ashamed to say that I didn't fight back. Not once. I have asked myself why not many times since. Maybe I thought I could appease him by not retaliating, unaware that he would perceive my passive reaction as a sign of guilt and become even more violent. At one point he hurled me against the marble fireplace and it's a miracle I didn't suffer a concussion. I don't remember how it ended because I blacked out. When I woke up the next morning, he was lying beside me. "Jesus, honey, I'm sorry," he said. "I don't know what got into me."

The sound of his voice filled me with terror and disgust. I was too terrified to speak.

"Do you think you can ever forgive me?" he said. "I swear it will never happen again."

He was right about that. It would never happen again because I would never see the bastard again. My lips felt cracked, I could barely see, and every part of me ached. I managed to hobble into the bathroom and when I looked in the mirror, I screamed. My face, swollen to three times its normal size, was unrecognizable. My eyes were tiny slits. My nose was stretched wide and flat. I wondered if it was broken. I was black and blue all over. It amazed me that I wasn't dead.

"I have to go to a hospital," I told him in as calm a voice as possible. "I'm going to call my doctor."

"Good idea. You might have internal injuries."

After I got Dr. LaRoe on the phone, I described my condition without identifying my assailant. I wasn't trying to protect Tom, only myself since I was afraid of retaliation if I admitted he had done this to me. Dr. LaRoe told me to come over immediately and when I walked into her office, her mouth dropped open.

"Who did zhis?" she asked, horrified. "It vas your ex-husband, vasn't it?"

Tom stood staunchly by my side, the concerned and solicitous boyfriend. Even in the safety of a physician's office, I was still afraid to point an accusing finger at him. I had never been so afraid of someone in my life.

"First vorms and now zhis!" Dr. LaRoe shook her head. "Vhat vill be next?"

She arranged for me to enter the Park East Hospital and to everyone's amazement, none of my bones were broken and there were no internal injuries. I stayed there for a week with bandages over my eyes, being fed through a tube. After the swelling had subsided, one of the nurses said that when I was admitted she thought I was a three-hundred-pound Japanese woman. Dr. LaRoe stopped by daily to see how I was doing and to press for the truth, convinced that John had attacked me. I vehemently denied it while at the same time refusing to say it was Tom, still fearful of repercussions.

Tom also came to see me every day. He sat at the edge of the bed, tears glistening in his eyes as he begged me to forgive him. "I forgive you," I lied, nearly choking on the words. "Why did you do it?"

"I was sure you had made love to your ex-husband earlier that day. I was jealous. I was afraid of losing you."

"Nothing happened between John and me but even if it had, do you think that would justify a brutal beating?"

"No, of course not. I realize now that I was wrong. Nothing like this will ever happen again, I promise. I'll never doubt you again."

He would never doubt *me?* I wanted to laugh, but it hurt too much. I wanted to cry, attack him, kill him. I hated him and wished he were dead. The sight of him revolted me. My only consolation was that someday I would be able to use this sordid experience in a book. Yes, even in times of despair the novelist's brain is forever churning and when Dr. LaRoe asked if she could bring me anything from my apartment, I requested the manuscript of *Getting Rid of Richard*. By then the bandages were off my eyes and I wanted to get back to work.

It made me feel better to be writing again, albeit in longhand, as it helped alleviate the depression and confusion I couldn't seem to shake no matter how hard I tried. That I could have become involved with a monster like Tom made me doubt my own judgment, even though I kept telling myself there was no way I could have foreseen where his pathological jealousy would lead. That I hadn't fought back was another source of anguish and self-condemnation. What was wrong with me? How could I have been so clueless? So spineless? I hadn't yet learned that it was a mistake to blame the victim.

"You vill be able to go home tomorrow," Dr. LaRoe said one afternoon. "You are lucky to haf such a nice boyfriend."

The last thing I intended to do was let Tom come home with me and I told him so later that day. "It's over between us. I never want to see you again."

"You can't mean that." His face wore a pained expression. "I'll make it up to you, honey. I'll never raise my hand to you again. Give me another chance, I beg you."

"No."

"Please."

"No."

"I love you."

"No."

"I need you."

For what? Batting practice? "No."

"I want to marry you."

"No!"

I was not as fearless as I sounded because I knew that once back home I would never feel safe. The brownstone I lived in was very accessible, the lock on the vestibule door so flimsy that a child could have gotten in. I shuddered at the image of Tom racing up the stairs and pounding on my door late one night or calling me on the phone, threatening harm if I didn't accede to his demands. The only solution was to get rid of the apartment and temporarily drop out of sight. I was even afraid to go back to work until I felt sure that Tom was out of my life for good.

I called Wade, saying that I had been in an automobile accident and was going to stay with my father in the Bronx while I recuperated. Wade was very solicitous and promised that my job would be waiting when I returned. Tom was nowhere in sight the morning I left the hospital, but only because I had lied to him about the date of my discharge. I stopped by my apartment long enough to pack a suitcase and arrange for the phone to be disconnected. Then I took the subway to my father's. When he questioned me about the fading bruises on my face, I gave him the same story about an automobile accident and spent the next few days resting, writing, trying to come to terms with what happened.

Since my father was at work during the day, I had long stretches of peaceful time in which to restore myself both physically and emotionally. Still I knew that for the rest of my life I would bear scars resulting from Tom's brutal attack, not on my face or body, but in my soul. Certain experiences change us forever, they challenge our faith. I would never again be the same trusting person I had been before, yet I didn't want to become hard and cynical either. I wanted to learn from the experience and hopefully turn it into something positive, although what that "something" might be I had no idea.

When I felt strong enough to cope, I began looking for a new apartment and found one on West 16th Street. It didn't have a working fireplace or a desk built into the wall by John Howard Lawson, but the price and location were right so I took it. In arranging for telephone service, I made sure that my number would be unlisted. Not long after I moved in, Tom called me at the office.

"I've missed you," he said. "Can't we get together for a drink?"

The sound of his voice acted as instant replay of what he had done to me. "Not for a drink, not for anything. It's over. Don't call me again." I slammed down the receiver, trembling.

Several months later I ran into Alan Abrons in Bloomingdale's and told him the whole story. To my surprise, he wasn't shocked. "You're not the first gal Tom has gotten physical with and I doubt if you'll be the last," he coolly said. "You should talk to his ex-wife and the woman he was involved with before you."

He mentioned their names. They were both successful actresses (one on Broadway, one in the movies) and while I could empathize with what they must have gone through, I felt relieved to know that Tom had a history of violence. It meant I wasn't an isolated case and wasn't to blame. I had been dealing with a pathologically jealous and insecure man who, no matter what I did or didn't do, was bound to explode sooner or later. "It wasn't your fault," I kept telling myself. "You were innocent. Innocent. Innocent."

In time I picked up the pieces of my life and went on. I continued to work at Fairchild Publications. I met other men, but trusting them was as difficult as I had imagined. Once when a gentle soul reached out to remove a speck of dirt from my collar, I flinched thinking he was going to hit me. There were no counseling services or support groups for battered women in those days, so unless you could afford private therapy you were on your own.

After I finished *Getting Rid of Richard*, Sterling Lord agreed to be my agent. It was the best news I had had in a long time and a few months later I started my second novel. Three pages at a time.

A Tale of Five Cities

Acapulco: 1954

TODAY it's a famous resort, but when I first laid eyes on it in 1954 it was a small sleepy town with only a few luxury hotels located on or near Caleta, the morning beach. Homos, the afternoon beach—a long shimmering stretch of sand and sea—was devoid of housing of any kind and construction on the new Hilton Hotel had been mysteriously abandoned at the eighth floor.

What were we doing in Acapulco that sunny October, I kept wondering whenever I thought about our limited funds? I refer to my husband, myself, our best friend Harvey Anhalt (who had driven down with us from New York), and Mike the Englishman whom we'd picked up at a bar in Mexico City. On the other hand, Acapulco wasn't expensive back then. The four of us managed to rent a two-bedroom house not far from the afternoon beach for fifty dollars a month. I still remember the address: Uno Calle del Tigre. Today it probably costs fifty dollars a minute to live at One Tiger Street, which still doesn't explain what we were doing in Acapulco.

It started with the moving company that my husband, John Elbert, and I owned. At first, we couldn't decide on an appropriate name for this fly-by-night operation until after considering all the typical names for moving companies, I came up with "The Hysterical Movers: if you don't call us, we'll scream!" It was so goofy that we both loved it and I placed an ad in *The Villager*, a local weekly newspaper. (*The Village Voice* had not yet come into existence.) Uninsured, unlicensed by the Public Service Commission, and totally illegal, The Hysterical Movers proved to be a veritable goldmine. We paid our workers minimum wage, which was more than we paid the IRS. To put it simply, we had no overhead, no office, no garage, no expenses other than gasoline for the four vehicles we ended up owning: a large van, a smaller van known as "The Greek," a panel truck and a Pontiac station wagon for beach runs.

My husband and I were living in Greenwich Village, on Thompson Street to be exact, in a twenty-five-dollar-a-month cold-water flat which served as our headquarters. This meant that I sat home booking moving jobs and listening to customers' complaints, while John paid off the workers at the Minetta Tavern on MacDougal Street, a few blocks away. John drank and conducted all business at Minetta's. The men we hired to work for us were our friends, none of whom knew anything about moving furniture, at least not at the beginning. They were struggling writers, painters, poets, actors and musicians, all anxious to make a fast buck.

There was a Norwegian sculptor who used to show up for work in a long flowing cape and rope-tied sandals, a frail flutist who didn't look strong enough to lift a canvas chair, a part-time English professor with shoulder-length hair and beer bottle eyeglasses, an actor with a matinee idol profile, a black piano player with failing eyesight (he drove). Since we paid the men in cash as soon as the job was completed and didn't deduct withholding tax, we had no trouble finding willing if incompetent help. Afterward the men got plastered at Minetta's and talked about how they had angled a double refrigerator down a narrow winding staircase, or nearly collapsed on a six-flight walkup carrying five rooms of solid mahogany furniture, eighty-nine book cartons, and an upright piano.

We paid drivers one dollar and fifty cents an hour, helpers one dollar and twenty-five cents. A two-man job cost the client eight dollars an hour. A three-man job cost thirteen-fifty an hour. We accepted no checks and since there were no credit cards back then, this was strictly a cash and carry operation. You can see the financial possibilities. At the beginning when we only owned The Greek, which my husband bought for a hundred dollars on a boozy late night bet, he used to do the driving himself to save money. That he later squandered the profits on vodka martinis at Minetta's didn't seem contradictory to him.

"We don't have a garage," was how he justified his actions. "So it all evens out."

"No, it doesn't," I said. "We're starting to get parking tickets and they're expensive."

"Not if you don't pay them."

That was a new one on me. "Won't we get into trouble?"

"They'd have to catch us first."

Ultimately it was his blithe disregard for parking tickets that led to our winding up in Acapulco a year later, but at the time I admired his nonchalant attitude since I tended to be a worrier. When we were late to a job because one of our workers had overslept, I worried about every subsequent job being equally late. When a customer said we had broken a leg off his Parson's table, I worried about her reporting us to the Public Service Commission. When a job estimated a four hours ran to six, I worried that the customer would refuse to pay. When I saw John drinking up all our profits night after night, I worried about our financial future.

"The money goes from a client's pocket straight into your vodka martini," I complained when we were still struggling along with only The Greek. "We're not saving anything."

"It doesn't matter because I just bought three new vehicles: a large van, a panel truck and a station wagon. The Hysterical Movers are now the largest movers in Greenwich Village and soon to become the most prosperous."

I was flabbergasted. "Where did you get the money?"

"From our silent partner. Bill Dawson is a rich kid who's so impressed with *la vie boheme* that he decided to invest in us. I think what really grabbed him is that his father is an ultraconservative corporation lawyer and we're mavericks. It's Bill's way of spitting at the establishment." John smiled triumphantly. "He put up all the money, but the vehicles are registered in my name."

"Bill Dawson sounds familiar."

"We moved him last month from the Upper East Side down to

Waverly Place. He loved being moved by an art historian and a ballet dancer instead of the usual muscle-bound goons."

This was an unexpected turn of events. "I guess with four vehicles, we'll finally have to get a garage."

"I don't see why," my husband said.

Until then I was only moderately busy booking moving jobs and could look forward to the quiet evening hours when I sat down at the typewriter and picked up the thread of whatever short story I was working on at the moment. I had been writing these stories and trying unsuccessfully to get them published for several years. In between stories I now decided to revise our ad for The Hysterical Movers pointing out that we owned more vehicles than any other company in the vicinity and were equipped to handle all jobs, from the smallest to the largest.

I placed this ad in several neighborhood newspapers as well as in *Show Business* since actors were forever relocating. Within a week my quiet evening hours were a thing of the past. The telephone never stopped ringing. Business was booming. People loved the name, The Hysterical Movers, which was at odds with the conventional names of our rivals, all of whose ads boasted that they were bonded, insured and licensed. We avoided these claims mostly because they weren't true, but also because our outlaw stance was applauded in nonconformist Greenwich Village. Clients beamed when we arrived at a job site with a motley-looking crew of bright, well-educated men who criticized their paintings and debated the virtues of Tolstoy versus Dostoevsky, Billie Holiday versus Dinah Washington.

If one of our movers scratched or broke a piece of furniture, I would promptly dispatch our "art restorer" to take care of the problem. This was Bobby Longstreet, a talented painter who drank boilermakers in the morning and arrived at the customer's home with a makeshift kit containing shoe dye, oil paints and some minor tools. Charming and well-spoken, if slightly snockered, Billy managed to pacify the customer by relating stories of his privileged childhood in Newport as he diligently repaired the damage. Amazing as it sounds, nobody ever threatened to sue us because of damages—or for any other reason, either.

Once when we were doing an evening job, the customers, a young affluent couple, decided to leave while the movers were still packing up their belongings, saying they would meet them at the new apartment uptown in a little while. That was fine with our three men, who finished a few hours later and were ready to depart when they realized that the worksheet containing the new address was nowhere to be found. Since the telephone was disconnected, one of them ran downstairs to a public phone booth to call me but I wasn't home, having decided to join John at Minetta's for a late dinner. (There were no answering machines back then.)

I had realized that if I didn't take a nightly break, I would go crazy trapped in that small apartment with the constantly-ringing phone and so while I was enjoying my veal piccata, the three movers were wondering what to do next. They knew that the young couple was probably sitting in their new empty apartment thinking we had absconded with all of their furniture, books, paintings, and every piece of clothing they owned. I didn't get home until well past midnight, by which time, unbeknownst to me, the movers had finished off a fifth of Scotch that the young couple so generously provided and were passed out in the empty flat, leaving the fully-loaded van locked up downstairs. It was only at daybreak that they managed to reach me and when they finally got to the new address, twelve hours late, the bleary eyed couple was thrilled to see them.

"Where have you been?" the wife cried. "We were worried sick."

"We couldn't find the worksheet with your new address," the driver informed them. "After looking everywhere, we figured that one of you must have picked it up by mistake. That's what happened, isn't it?"

"Well, I don't have it," the husband said.

"Neither do I," his wife concurred.

"Worksheets don't disappear, M'am. Maybe you should check your purse." To her astonishment, there it was. She couldn't believe it "I don't understand—"

"Stranger things have happened in the heat of moving," the driver said. "But I'm afraid we'll have to charge you for those hours we lost."

Her husband cut in. "Now just a minute. Surely you don't mean we have to pay for twelve extra hours."

"That's what you should do, but why don't we split the difference? Call it six extra hours in addition to the four we spent doing the job."

The husband handed over one hundred and thirty-five dollars plus a ten dollar tip. As the movers were leaving, they could hear the wife saying, "I still don't understand how that worksheet got in my purse."

Two of the movers, who knew they hadn't put it there, turned to the third guy, the Norwegian sculptor with the rope-tied sandals. He smiled sheepishly. "I needed the extra dough. Don't tell John."

"Why not?" the driver laughed. "He'd probably congratulate you."

When I heard what happened, I warned the Norwegian sculptor that if he ever did something like that again, he would be fired. We may have been uninsured, unlicensed, and flagrantly illegal but we still had our principles.

I couldn't believe the amount of money that began to roll in, nor could I believe how quickly it rolled out again thanks to John's penchant for vodka martinis. If I expected our flush of success to fuel his ambition and moderate his drinking, I was wrong. In fact the more that business thrived, the less interested in it he became. Whereas in the past he used to drive The Greek himself, now he couldn't seem to get out of bed before noon. Since he had closed the bars at four a.m., this wasn't surprising but it did wreak havoc with our schedules as he stubbornly insisted on appointing himself driver for the very first job, usually slated for seven a.m.

"You know that you'll never get up in time," I would repeatedly warn him. "Let me hire someone to take that time slot."

"No, I'll do it."

The next morning would be a repeat of the morning before, with the first job delayed while I frantically called our workers trying to find another driver. This meant that all subsequent jobs using the same vehicle were delayed, and after a while I became tired of listening to angry customers demanding to know what had happened to the movers.

"You're ruining this business," I finally told John, who upon awakening at noon would spend the next few hours drinking coffee and staring off into space, no doubt recovering from a fierce hangover before disappearing into the boozy confines of Minetta's. "From now on I plan to forget about you as a driver, worker, or anything else of value. Just keep out of my way and I'll keep out of yours."

"Who's going to drive in the morning?"

"Ted Peters." Ted was one of our most experienced workers and a good friend, to boot. "I've promised him a steady weekly wage to take over, and he's accepted."

"You should have consulted me."

"When? When you're not asleep, you're drinking your brains out. When should I have consulted you?"

Ted Peters' wife, Lynn, dropped by one evening. She was pregnant with their first child and after thanking me for having ensured Ted a steady salary, she said, "Don't you wonder where John is all those late nights?"

"I know where he is. At a bar."

"Aren't you afraid he might be involved with another woman?"

"A vodka martini. That's what he's involved with."

"You seem awfully sure about that."

"I am sure. I understand my husband's priorities."

I had been with John, on and off, for five years by then and although he was drinking heavily when I met him in 1949, I didn't take it seriously. For one thing, I knew next to nothing about alcoholism, my only first hand experience being a maternal uncle named

Arbie who was a Skid Row rummy, much to my mother's embarrassment and my father's derision. The difference between Arbie and John, at least in my mind, was that Arbie looked and acted like a hardcore drunk: deeply depressed, riddled with guilt, always smelling of cheap whiskey and ashamed of it. I can't remember John smelling of anything other than cigarette tobacco, in addition to which he looked and acted like he was having a good time with no guilt or shame involved. I didn't realize that alcoholism came in many different guises, but that ultimately the disease was the same and if unchecked would land the addict in the grave, jail or the nuthouse.

The other reason I wasn't alarmed by John's drinking at the beginning was because it seemed glamorous and exciting. Since neither of my parents indulged, I was in rebellion against what I perceived to be their joyless existence. I don't think my mother ever tasted alcohol in her life and my father only threw back a fast schnapps at a celebratory occasion, like a wedding or bar mitzvah. Otherwise, forget it. I can still see the distinctive bottle of Johnny Walker that was relegated to the top shelf of our coat closet where it lay buried beneath scarves and hats, to be taken down when the building superintendent performed some task that required a tip. Instead of money my mother gave him a shot of Scotch and after he left, she would mutter the word, "*shicker*" under her breath. It means "drunk" in Yiddish and is always said with the utmost contempt. Jews back than had no use for anyone who drank.

The only other person for whom Johnny Walker came down from the closet was my uncle Nat, Arbie's younger brother. Nat showed up in New York once a year bringing gifts for all of us and spreading some much-needed cheer during the bleak Depression years. Nat drank socially, gracefully, and like my future husband seemed to enjoy it with no ill effects. Since I had always been enamored of Nat who was devilishly handsome, lived in San Francisco, and ran around with gorgeous showgirls (one of whom he married on a bet), I not only approved of everything he did, but considered it the thing to do. Obviously throwing back a few drinks of hard liquor was the thing to do. I might add that in later years Nat stopped drinking altogether because of a medical condition. Not being an alcoholic, he was able to abstain. John was another story, but it took me a long time to realize it.

After I hired Ted Peters, John's contribution to The Hysterical Movers became reduced to the tearing up of parking tickets, which by now were pouring in by the carload. The initial fine was five dollars a ticket, but if it wasn't paid within a week it increased to ten dollars. After a month, it became twenty-five dollars. During the next six months, we accumulated approximately one hundred and twenty-five parking tickets, all of which John cavalierly threw away. That, all by itself, would have been a foolhardy thing to do but there was an added factor, which made it downright insane.

The added factor was John Murtagh, Chief Justice of the New York Supreme Court who had decided to wage a one-man war against scofflaws and fine them double, often triple the amount of their incremented tickets. In some cases as further punishment, he sent them to prison on Riker's Island for six months. (Ten years later, John Murtagh would be the presiding judge at the landmark Lenny Bruce obscenity case.) "If Murtagh catches up with us, we'll have to pay close to ten thousand dollars," I told John. At the time, that was like one hundred thousand today. "And don't forget the possible jail sentence."

"Murtagh will never find me and if by some fluke he does, we'll unload the three trucks and take off for Mexico in the station wagon."

This was the first I'd heard of the Mexico escape plan and I was horrified. "Leaving the country under those circumstances would be a felony. What's in Mexico?"

"Peace. Tranquility. Easy living. It's where I could write my novel." He had been talking about this novel for as long as I'd known him. "Besides, it's time to get out of the rat race."

"Not if it means committing a felony."

"It won't come to that," my fearless husband assured me.

But it almost did.

Around this time we became chummy with a young lawyer named David O'Keefe, who had been an Army pilot in the Second World War. The way we met was simple if dramatic. John and I were guests at a beach house on Fire Island one weekend when literally, out of the blue, a four-seater Cessna landed beside our window and out stepped David. I think he was running low on gas. David and John struck up an immediate friendship as John had been a Navy pilot. When we told David about Murtagh and the parking tickets, he said to be sure to contact him if the law ever descended upon us and he would take care of everything. That made me feel a little better.

Meanwhile John started looking at maps of Mexico and had become enthused about a remote fishing village south of Guadalajara. It was called Lake Chapala and reputed to be picturesque as well as dirt cheap. "I'll bet we could live there for six months on what we spend in one month in New York," he said, wistfully.

"Not if you continue drinking vodka martinis at the same rate of speed."

He regarded me as if I were mentally retarded. "You don't drink vodka in Mexico. You drink tequila. It's so cheap, they practically give it away."

A few weeks later we were out on the town, midtown Manhattan, to be exact. In the back of the station wagon were two lawyers from Chicago and in another car were Ted and Lynn Peters. The six of us were headed for a French bistro in the West Fifties and afterward we planned to take the visiting lawyers to hear Dizzy Gillespie at Basin Street. John was driving too fast when suddenly, the sound of police sirens filled the air.

"Slow down," I said.

His response was to accelerate.

"What are you doing?" one of the lawyers cried, as the sirens grew louder.

"I'm going to outrace them."

"Are you crazy?"

He managed to get up to sixty mph by the time the cops caught up with us. What happened as a result shouldn't be hard to guess. A speeding ticket prompted the investigation into other possible violations by the same vehicle and that's when the parking tickets came spilling out, but because there were no computers in those days only thirty-eight tickets for the station wagon were unearthed. The cops didn't know that an additional eighty-seven tickets garnered by our three other vehicles were still outstanding.

"This is no laughing matter," one of the lawyers said at dinner. "I hope you realize that, John."

"You guys worry too much. That's your problem."

"You're the one with a problem, John."

Not long afterward a cop showed up at our apartment. Having anticipated his visit, John made a dash for the bedroom window, ran down the fire escape and into the kitchen of the Gran Ticino restaurant beneath us, grabbed an apron and began cooking pasta. When the cop came barreling through, the staff pointed toward the front door. They were sympathetic to our plight, John being one of their steady martini customers. After he removed the apron and thanked everyone for their help, he came upstairs to tell me and our friend, Harvey Anhalt, what had transpired.

"What are you going to do?" Harvey asked.

"Hightail it out of the country as soon as possible."

Several evenings later when we were coming home from Minetta's, a plainclothesman nabbed John as he unlocked the door to our flat. "Are you John Elbert?"

"No, I'm Harvey Anhalt."

"Let me see your driver's license."

"I don't have it on me."

"I'll wait while you go get it."

My husband looked wildly around, but this time no escape was possible. "What if I am John Elbert?" he said.

"We want you to come downtown for questioning."

"Just questioning?"

"You'll be back before you know it."

"Find David O'Keefe," were John's departing words to me. "*Fast.*"

David O'Keefe was not so easily found, I discovered the next morning when John still hadn't returned. It was Saturday. I tried calling David at his home and office but to no avail. (Cell phones were years off in the future.) I couldn't imagine where he was and started to feel as hysterical as the name of our company. Without David to represent John, I felt sure that he would end up on Riker's Island. I cried on the shoulder of our silent partner, Bill Dawson, who had begun to wonder whether investing in a shady Village moving company was such a smart idea after all.

"I haven't seen a cent of profits in over six months," he told me.

I tried to hide my astonishment. "What was John's explanation?"

"That there weren't any profits, but I don't see how that's possible."

While I didn't say it, neither did I.

"Your husband is a con man," Bill Dawson continued. "A charming con man, but a con man nonetheless. He said that if I was unhappy with our arrangement, I should complain to the Better Business Bureau. I hope Murtagh throws the book at the devious son of a bitch."

A handful of moving jobs were scheduled for that weekend and in between trying to locate David O'Keefe, I gave truck keys and worksheets to drivers, answered the usual customers' complaints, booked future jobs and netted over three hundred dollars, which made me wonder if it was such a bad idea to let John go to jail. It would keep him off the sauce, maybe even give him a new respect for the law and without him to guzzle up all the profits, I could save a pile of money to boot.

Every Sunday I would bake a cake and go visit my convict husband on Riker's Island where I would tell him how great business was and how much money I had deposited in our savings account. It was a gratifying fantasy, but ultimately unenforceable. Con man or not, marriage in trouble or not, I couldn't let John go to jail. I loved the guy.

Meanwhile I kept receiving frantic messages from John to get him out on bail. Every mover in the Village called that weekend, pleading with me to accede to his wishes. They claimed that as a woman I couldn't appreciate the barbaric conditions under which he was being held prisoner in the Tombs and if I had an ounce of compassion, I would post bail. Much as I wanted to, I didn't dare risk it because of John's threat to flee the country. I urged him to sit tight and said I would see him Monday morning when he was scheduled to face the punitive Judge Murtagh with David O'Keefe in tow. Another twenty-four hours of dogged telephone calls ensued before I remembered that David kept his plane hangared at the Westchester Airport. To my relief, that was where I finally located him.

"I'll meet you at the courthouse tomorrow morning," he said. "Bring a razor and change of clothes for John. Don't' wear lipstick or any makeup. Dress simply."

"No makeup?"

"I want the two of you to look like an innocent, clean cut, young American couple. Got it? What year was John in the Pacific?"

"What does the Pacific have to do with this?"

"Everything. John told me he saw action there. What year was it?"

"I'm not sure, I didn't know him then. Near the end of the war, I think, 1944 or 1945."

"Good. And by the way, you were smart not to have posted bail. It will sit well with Murtagh."

That evening several movers called back to wish me luck and say they had made bets on John's fate. The odds of him going to Riker's Island were heavy, Murtagh's past sentencing record being what it was. We all planned to convene at Minetta's the following day, either to celebrate or commiserate.

"At least Murtagh doesn't know about the tickets for the three trucks," Harvey Anhalt said. "John would really be up the creek if those came to light."

"It's where he deserves to be," Ted Peters chimed in. He and John had never gotten along. "The jerk has singlehandedly bankrupted a beautiful operation."

By the time David and I got John spruced up the next day, he looked as innocent as a spring lamb. With his straight blond hair, clean-shaven face, buttoned-down oxford blue shirt and freshly-pressed chinos, no one would believe that this was a man who had torn up one hundred and twenty-five parking tickets or was ready to jump bail and disappear into the tropics of Mexico.

"I've saved you from becoming an outlaw," I said when he chastised me for not getting him out on bail. "Someday you'll thank me."

"Don't hold your breath."

Just before we entered Judge Murtagh's private chambers, David O'Keefe cautioned us. "Keep your mouths shut, both of you. Let me do all the talking."

We nodded, wondering what he had in mind. John Murtagh was a tall, dark, saturnine man who kept his eyes assiduously averted from ours. He sat behind an impressive desk, a stenographer at his side. We sat opposite him. You could have cut the tension with a knife.

"I'm here more as John's friend than his lawyer," David O'Keefe tentatively began. "John is a struggling young novelist who, in order to support himself and his wife, bought a station wagon to do some light moving jobs. However he used poor judgment in the men he hired to work for him. Instead of telling John about the parking tickets they kept receiving, they secretly tore them up. It was only as a result of the recent unfortunate speeding violation that John became aware of what was going on behind his back all these months."

David sounded reasonable, convincing. It could have happened that way, I thought, wondering if Murtagh believed him but it was impossible to tell. Not once during David's earnest plea did the judge look up or register any facial expression whatsoever.

"I can personally vouch for John's good character," David went on. "He and I first met in San Diego at the end of 1944. We had both just returned from active combat in the Pacific. I was an Army pilot and John was flying TBMs for the Navy."

At that Murtagh suddenly stiffened, his eyed blinked, and he stared at John with sharp interest. Something significant had happened, but I couldn't imagine what. Only later did we learn what David knew all along: Murtagh had been a Naval officer himself. It was a clear-cut case of the good old boys' network not turning on one of its own. There was no question of John being sent to prison. Nor did Murtagh take the opportunity to double or triple his fines, as we had feared. Even the stenographer looked stunned when he said we only had to pay the original five dollars a ticket, but he would have to revoke John's driver's license for a year. After handing over a check for one hundred and ninety dollars, we were free to leave.

"In the future be careful who you hire to drive that station wagon," Judge Murtagh warned my husband.

"I will, Your Honor. Thank you."

Once we were out of earshot, John turned to me. "Start packing for Mexico. If that guy ever finds those other eighty-seven tickets, he'll put me away forever."

"How are we going to get to Mexico? You don't have a license." And I didn't drive back then.

"No sweat," he said as we strolled out of the courthouse. "I know a shyster lawyer who'll forge one for me."

When we headed for Mexico a few weeks later with a forged driver's license, Harvey Anhalt, and all our worldly possessions, we intended our final destination to be Lake Chapala and the frugal life. We didn't have much money, only a few thousand dollars that we'd gotten from selling Bill Dawson's three trucks. Bill had no idea we were liquidating our assets and skipping town.

"This will be a good lesson for him," was the way John summed it up. "It will knock that *la vie boheme* crap right out of his head. Actually he should be grateful to me for opening his eyes to the real world."

"Somehow I don't think he's going to feel very grateful when he realizes that you swindled him."

Harvey Anhalt didn't have any money at all. John agreed to cover his expenses after I secretly crept up to Harvey's apartment one evening and begged him to accompany is. "I can't face the trip alone with John," I said. "Things are very strained between us. If I had any guts, I would file for divorce right now, but I'm dying to see Mexico. I might not get another chance."

"I'm dying to see it too, but where will I keep my insulin?" Harvey was a diabetic. "It's supposed to be refrigerated."

"What happens if it isn't?"

He giggled fiendishly. "I have a lot of insulin shocks and turn into Dracula."

"We can buy an ice chest and put it in back of the station wagon. Then when we get to Chapala, we'll rent a house with a fridge. Will you come?"

"Sure, if John pays."

John was delighted to have Harvey along since I don't think he wanted to be alone with me any more than I wanted to be alone with him. We drove through the Lincoln Tunnel, swung onto the New Jersey Turnpike, and headed south. For some reason, we never did buy the ice chest and Harvey did end up having a lot of insulin shocks during the long journey. He told me to stick a sugar cube in his mouth the minute I saw him moaning and foaming, and not to be concerned. After the first few shocks didn't kill or incapacitate him, John and I stopped worrying about their recurrence. We pretended Harvey was a horse.

As we barreled through one state after another, never knowing where we would wind up that night, a vagabond mentality began to engulf us. We felt free, unencumbered, defiant in our Levi jeans which at that time were worn primarily by construction workers who prized their sturdiness and durability. (The days of designer jeans were years off.) At the Howard Johnson restaurants where we often stopped for meals, traditionally-clad people regarded us with a mixture of confusion and fear. We weren't playing the game and they knew it. We knew it too, reveled in it. It was 1954 and we were on the road while the rest of Eisenhower America was conscientiously launching suburban togetherness.

Within days of leaving New York, we found ourselves in the heart of the Deep South, a region with its own laws and lingo. We traveled through rural terrain populated by pale, washed-out looking men and women often living in miserable shacks, their children running around half naked. These people hadn't seen many outsiders and stared at us as though we were from another galaxy. John and Harvey had long hair, I had short hair, plus women didn't wear pants back then. Once when we stopped at a tiny sandwich shop, the proprietor looked so frightened that she said she didn't have any sandwiches. I pointed to the blackboard over the counter, which listed the different kinds.

"How about a ham and cheese?" I asked. "In fact, how about three of them?"

That I spoke English, albeit with a Northern accent, seemed to reassure her. "Okay."

Liquor laws were wildly erratic in the South, varying not only from state to state but from county to county. We never knew what to expect. On Knoxville's main drag, John turned to a crusty old-timer and asked where we could get a drink. It was after dark and we'd been driving all day.

"Son," the man drawled, spitting out a stream of tobacco juice, "this burg is as dry as the Mohave Desert."

A few counties farther on, we were served tall frosty Mint Juleps in the parking lot of an attractive Chinese restaurant. In our car, to be exact. It seemed that was the only place the restaurant could legally provide alcoholic beverages to its customers. Once in a luncheonette in Alabama, we noticed the waitress removing a tiny individual bottle of bourbon from behind the counter and placing it in front of a customer, who proceeded to open it and pour it into his empty water glass. Upon questioning, the waitress said that she could sell hard liquor but wasn't allowed to open the bottle herself.

Wherever we went, Jim Crow laws were starkly in evidence. Even though I knew they existed, I was shocked by each new reminder. In New Orleans as I bent down to drink from a public water fountain, I suddenly noticed the small bronze plaque: FOR WHITES ONLY. There was something sad and defeated and crazy about the South. Harvey said it was because they had lost the Civil War.

"They've never gotten over it. Haven't you noticed how many statues of Lee and Stonewall Jackson there are everywhere you turn? 'Let us cross over the river and rest under the trees.'"

"What's that?"

"Jackson's dying words."

Harvey was a Civil War buff.

Throughout the trip, we tried our best to economize. Our money was going to have to last until John finished his novel and we returned to New York where he would try to get it published. In retrospect it's obvious that we were being highly impractical and unrealistic about our financial situation, but when you're in your twenties you think you can do anything.

John liked to drive at night because he could make better time that way. We devoured miles of land while off in the distance neon signs beckoned and headlights of cars on the other side of the road blinded my eyes. Mostly we slept in the back of the station wagon and ate in cheap cafés. I remember the three of us waking up early on a cold gray morning somewhere in Mississippi, and trudging a few yards to a greasy spoon for breakfast. Our scrambled eggs were accompanied by a white wet mound of something unfamiliar looking.

"What is it?" I asked the waitress, whose flaming red hair was set in pink plastic curlers.

"You folks must be from up North. Them's grits, honey!"

At Laredo we crossed the border into Mexico and an instant change of atmosphere. It was like going from a somber listless world to one filled with laughter, abandon and a surrealist madcap energy. Yet beneath the laughter lurked a despair so extreme that it threw off an electrical charge all its own. For the first time in my life, I had a sensation of being where I truly belonged.

The Pan American Highway had been built by then but wasn't yet open for traffic, so after Nuevo Laredo we were routed through every small pueblo not on the map. Tourism was a bare trickle in Mexico in those days and in one village the people lined up outside their shops to watch us walk down Main Street. It was a little like *High Noon* comedy style as these villagers had never seen blue eyes, blond hair, sandy hair (Harvey), or a woman with short auburn hair wearing a man's shirt and jeans. After a few minutes of dead silence, they broke into raucous laughter, pointing at us and gesticulating wildly. To show our good will, we bought straw sombreros and continued our stroll. This apparition reduced them to another fit of uncontrollable laughter.

"*Como parezco?*" I asked several giggling señoras.

They were stunned that I could speak Spanish.

"*Ridicula*," one of them replied before collapsing into another bout of hysterics.

("How do I look?" "Ridiculous.")

In another village, the "mayor" grandly opened his home to us for the night. It was a mud hut with an earthen floor and no plumbing of any kind. The "mayor" and his wife treated us with great courtesy and consideration. The next morning as we stepped over their three sleeping children, we thanked them for their hospitality.

Although we realized that stopping off in Mexico City would be insanely expensive, who could resist?

John was anxious to see the world's largest bullring while Harvey and I were aching for a soft bed and some creature comforts after the rigors of the road. What I remember most vividly about Mexico City were the pyramids that stretched to the sky, the intoxicating quality of bullfights on Sunday afternoon, mariachi bands serenading us at native restaurants, and Indian women squatting outside the sparkling new Hilton Hotel patting their tortillas into shape as Spanish women in furs and jewels glided by, long black hair on their nylon legs peeking through. It turned out that hirsuteness was a sign of caste in Mexico, Indians being traditionally hairless.

We checked into a modest hotel in the downtown Juarez section of town, but naïvely left most of our suitcases in the back of the Pontiac station wagon since it didn't have a trunk. Every evening for the next week, an enterprising Mexican kid would ask John if he could "washa the car." John always agreed and gave him a peso. The day before we were due to leave for Lake Chapala, John was in a bad mood and told the kid to go washa his ears.

The next morning I was the first one to reach the station wagon, but when I looked in back I saw it was empty, all of our suitcases gone, stolen. One of them contained every short story I had ever written, as well as years of notes and research for my husband's long-delayed novel. I felt dizzy, weak. Turning mutely to John who had just walked up, I shook my head in despair but to my surprise he didn't register the tiniest bit sign of alarm or grief. "There's only one thing to do in a situation like this," he coolly announced, as Harvey and our new English friend Mike stood by horrified. "Let's go to Acapulco."

I insisted that we go to the police first, having heard that in Mexico there was something called a "thieves' market." We were duly directed to the Servicio Secreto where I tried to bribe the head honcho into locating our suitcases. Later I found out that the bribe would have worked if I had been more direct, but I was afraid of offending *el jefe* so instead of putting the cash right on the table, I said we were willing to pay "a lot of money" to get our possessions back. I looked *el jefe* straight in the eye, hoping he understood my intent since I was speaking in Spanish. He smiled, expressed his sympathies, and promised to assign his best men to the case. We cooled our heels for a few days and when nothing turned up, took off for Acapulco. I didn't know it then, but it was the beginning of the end. Of our trip. Of my marriage.

The bars in Acapulco were open around the clock and except for the eight or so hours that John spent in bed asleep, he was either drinking, getting ready to drink, or recovering from drinking. At first I felt sorry for him, having lost all those notes, but after a month I asked why he didn't write a different novel or else try to reconstruct the original one from memory.

"I'll have to give it some thought," he said, sipping from an ever-present glass of tequila.

That was when I realized he was glad his notes had been stolen, as it gave him the perfect excuse to drown his sorrows. Not that he ever admitted it, but what else could account for his happy carefree attitude? I was still furious over the loss of my short stories and eager to start writing again. The house at Uno Calle del Tigre had a kitchenette, two bedrooms, and a long patio which served as living room, dining room and studio for me. In the quiet early morning hours while the others were still asleep, I put my portable typewriter on the dining table and worked on a new short story. The only reason my typewriter hadn't been stolen was because I'd brought it up to our room in the Mexico City hotel.

When the brood awakened, I was through with my day's stint and proceeded to cook an enormous breakfast. Being outdoors so much gave us all a hearty appetite. After breakfast we drove crosstown to Caleta, the morning beach, where we spent the day beneath a shaded table. This was a lively convivial spot with lots of people-watching going on. The majority of tourists were colorful types primarily from California and Texas, who had money to burn. Waiters passed by frequently taking orders for drinks and food. I drank Coca-Cola. Mike and Harvey drank Dos Equis beer. John drank tequila knockouts, a lethal combination of tequila, rum, grenadine and cheap brandy.

Periodically John, Mike and I ran down to the water to swim. Sometimes we rented a glass-bottomed boat and went out looking at submerged sea life. John even learned how to snorkel. Harvey not only couldn't swim, but had lost his bathing trunks in one of the stolen suitcases and refused to buy another pair. Except for two pairs of jeans and a pair of elegant silk pajamas from Sak's, he had lost all his clothes but accepted his plight philosophically. At the beach he wore jeans and in the early evening, when we relaxed on our patio watching iguanas race up and down the walls of the house, he wore the pajamas. They were a birthday gift from his sister, an interior decorator in New York.

Our one meal out was lunch, which we managed fairly inexpensively at the beachside restaurant. Even though I cooked breakfast and dinner at home, it didn't cost more than five dollars a week to feed the four of us. Hard to believe today, but true. I know because I kept a record of household expenses. Once when I tried to economize with hotdogs for dinner, the grocery bill rose. Hotdogs were more expensive in Mexico than the best cut of beef because they were a manufactured product. Items like coffee, bread and canned goods could be bought at a small Americanized shop in town, but for fresh fruits and veggies it was necessary to go to the open-air market. This was quite an experience.

The market had no refrigeration, no sanitation, and it stank. Beef liver hung in slabs under the broiling sun, with flies glued to it. People bought the liver, too. White cheese was covered with flies as well. In certain parts of the market there were restaurants where poor Mexicans could order rotten eggs cooked to order or a bowl of rancid soup. I happen to have a terrible sense of smell, but even I used to pinch my nose while scouting around for fruits and vegetables. If we got there late in the day, almost everything was spoiled, which didn't stop the owner of one stall from triumphantly biting into brown rotting lettuce and crying, "*Esta fresca!*" ("It's fresh!")

Dinnertime was a happy festive affair with the four of us tanned and glowing from a day at the beach. We ate lots of freshly caught fish, roasted meat and vegetables baked with pungent spices. I missed the green salads I'd become used to in New York, but we had been warned to stay away from anything raw that couldn't be peeled as a safeguard against dysentery. Sometimes a man came around selling venison, which had been killed in the nearby hills and was wonderful for stew. Cooking in a foreign country was an adventure I enjoyed a great deal. In fact I enjoyed everything about Acapulco except for the time spent alone with my husband, but fortunately that didn't amount to much. During the day we were with Harvey and Mike, and at night I went to bed early while John went barhopping. By the time he returned hours later, I was asleep or pretended to be. Our room had twin beds, so it was easy to avoid him.

After we had been in Acapulco for several months, a private investigator showed up one day and demanded to see Señor Anhalt. It seemed that Harvey's father had hired him to trace his son's whereabouts and bring him home ASAP. I don't know where the P.I. got his information, but he thought that John had a record for armed robbery and I was a flamenco dancer. After we stopped laughing, Harvey became melancholy. He didn't want to go back to New York and I didn't blame him since I'd never seen him so happy. The problem was he felt afraid to antagonize his father, who held the purse strings.

"Without the old man, I don't know where my next batch of insulin is coming from," he told us.

Mike, who had emigrated from England to work for a Rolls Royce dealership in Toronto, found the three of us very amusing. He used to call me "Chicquita Banana" pronounced "Bah-nah-nah," and suggested that Harvey get a job so he could be financially independent.

"I'm too jaded for gainful employment," Harvey said, smiling at the prospect. He was twenty-eight and would be dead within six years from diabetic complications.

After the private investigator whisked him off to New York, it wasn't long before Mike announced that his holiday time had run out and he was returning to Canada. John and I were desolate to see both men go, not only because we valued their companionship but because it meant being alone with each other. Our days quickly turned into the worst kind of tedium. We ate breakfast, went to the morning beach, swam in the bay, shopped in the smelly market, and watched iguanas in the evening, silent as two old Indians.

By now our marriage was at rock bottom and we were barely on speaking terms. If I thought John's drinking had been excessive in New York, it was nothing compared to the full-time occupation it became in Acapulco. He reeked of tequila and I couldn't stand for him to touch me. What for years had been a compelling sex life ground to a standstill. I suspected that while he was out barhopping at night, he satisfied his needs with other women, which was fine with me.

There was an unexpected and welcome break in our routine when at the beach, we met a middle-aged American businessman who asked if we would accompany him to the red light district. Tom needed our help because he didn't speak a word of Spanish and was afraid of getting fleeced by the local prostitutes. I confessed that I didn't realize Acapulco had a red light district.

"Oh, sure," Tom said. "They flourish legally all over Mexico."

We drove him there several nights later. The place was situated a few miles outside of town and as we approached paved streets gave way to deeply rutted roads. Even in the darkness, I could see couples copulating against the sides of ramshackle buildings. Bands of men roamed the area, shouting drunkenly and waving bottles of liquor in the air. While we continued driving toward the bright lights up ahead, small animals scurried away from our car (cats? rats? rabbits?). I suspected that the American West must have looked something like this a long time ago.

The house of prostitution was located inside a huge rambling dancehall that provided live entertainment and was open to the general public, men and women alike. The atmosphere was highly charged, pulsating, noisy, boisterous. If I hadn't known better, I would have taken it for a rowdy nightclub that just happened to have provocatively-dressed girls floating around. One of them came to our table and asked if she could join us. She was about seventeen, tall, slender, with large dark eyes, a lot of cleavage and a diffident manner. Her name was Maria and she spoke no English. Except for the few luxury hotels, nobody spoke English in Acapulco in 1954, not even the police. In addition to having studied it in high school and college, I boned up while we were driving down from New York with books I had brought along. Despite John and Harvey's initial skepticism, it came in handy especially when we had car trouble and I could tell Mexican auto mechanics what the problem was in Spanish. I still remember how to say the spark plugs are bad. *Las bujias estan malas.*

"Ask her how much she wants," Tom whispered in my ear.

"Don't you think it might be polite to offer her a drink first?"

"Sure, sure." He glanced around the cavernous room for a waiter and when he couldn't spot one, he began snapping his fingers and clapping his hands. Not that anyone could hear him above the roar of the music. "What's everybody having?"

John was having a tequila knockout, Tom was having a beer, Maria and I were having Coca-Cola. Soon she and I began talking as though we had chanced to meet on a double date. She wanted to know what my husband's name was, what he did for a living, where we lived in the United States, how long we'd been in Acapulco, how long we'd been married, whether we had children. After I obligingly filled her in, she said she had always wanted to visit New York. Was it as exciting as she heard? Was it easy to earn money there? Did she think she could get a job? I was hesitant to press her on what kind of job she meant, so I said "yes" to all her questions.

"Ask her how much," Tom repeated, more urgently now.

I told him to be patient.

"Who's your friend?" Maria inquired.

"He's a businessman from Houston and he finds you very attractive." I took a deep breath. "Are you interested?"

She lowered her eyes demurely and said she would have to think about it.

"*Ask her how much.*"

"I can't. It's too embarrassing."

"She's a whore! What do you mean, embarrassing? Ask her!" I told him that I would have to lead up to it, sorry I ever agreed to act as go-between. Meanwhile Maria was saying that she once fell in love with an American sailor who looked just like my husband. The sailor's name was John, too, she confided with a smile. It seemed obvious that she didn't care for Tom, who by now was staring at me in exasperation. After considerable verbal fumbling, I asked Maria how much. She winked and named some outrageous sum. When I repeated it, Tom choked on his beer.

"She's got to be kidding! For that kind of dough, I could get three whores. Are you sure you didn't misunderstand? All I want to do is get laid. I don't want any fancy stuff. Ask the bitch again what the real price is."

"I don't like him," Maria told me. "He has dishonest eyes."

"I don't like him either."

"*Tell the bitch to cut the crap and give me the real price.*"

I smiled at her. "My husband would like to dance with you. Is that okay?"

Her face lit up. She said she would love to.

"Go dance with her, then we're leaving," I said under my breath to John. "As far as I'm concerned, this jerk can stay here and negotiate on his own. I've had it."

As they moved toward the dance floor, Tom exploded. "Why the hell is she dancing with him? What are you trying to pull? If you and your husband are into threesomes, count me out. I'm just a normal guy who wants a little Mexican tail, but I'm not going to pay the ridiculous price you quoted. Are you sure you got that price right? When she comes back, write the figure down on paper so there's no misunderstanding."

He was still raving when they returned. I told Maria I was sorry, but we had to leave. She shook my hand and said it was a pleasure talking to me. John threw some pesos on the table and the two of us quickly headed for the door.

"Hey, where are you going?" Tom called out, galvanized by what was happening. "Hey, wait for me!"

John and I joined hands and walked faster.

"Don't leave me here! I don't speak Spanish! I don't have a car! Wait!"

Once outside, we raced for the station wagon before Tom could catch up with us and drove off, laughing. It was the first time in a long time we had been in accord about anything, but instead of drawing us closer it only served to remind us how far apart we had grown.

"We're almost broke," John informed me soon afterward. "We don't even have enough money to get back to New York."

"Why didn't you say so before?"

"I've been waiting for Harvey to come through with some dough. Before he left, he said he would try to hit his old man up for a loan but I guess he wasn't successful."

"What happens now?"

"Beats me."

In the end, John's parents sent us a nominal sum. By living on sandwiches and sleeping in back of the station wagon, we managed to make it to the border. In Dallas, we stayed with a man we had met in Acapulco. By then we were so broke that we couldn't afford repairs on the battered Pontiac, so we decided to sell it and use the money for plane tickets to New York. We placed a classified ad in the local paper, sat next to the telephone and waited. A few calls trickled in, but nobody made an offer. Days went by. Weeks. We played gin rummy to make the time go faster. We agreed that once home, we would file for divorce. It was a very civilized agreement, very quiet and unemotional. The reprimands, accusations, and general craziness would come later. For now, we were simply worn out.

Just as we were about to give up hope of ever unloading the car, a black Baptist minister bought it and we left Dallas the following afternoon. As our plane climbed into the sky, John said, "Whatever terrible things you may say about me in the future, you can't say that I didn't take you to exotic places."

Today whenever I see an ad describing Acapulco as a glamorous playground for the beautiful people, I remember Harvey sitting on the patio in his silk pajamas, Mike calling me "Chicquita Banana," but mostly I remember how we happened to get there in the first place—courtesy of The Hysterical Movers, one hundred and twenty-five parking tickets, and Judge John Murtagh. I often wonder if those other eighty-seven tickets ever showed up.

Paris: 1959

THE LAST TIME I saw Paris, its heart was definitely not young and gay. Bitter and disillusioned would be more like it. Wherever I went, I heard pointed remarks about *sals Americains* (dirty Americans) and caught the look of hostility on many a Frenchman's face. Since I didn't consider myself a typical tourist, I couldn't figure out what I had done to deserve such harsh treatment and the more I reviewed my behavior, the more confused I became.

I tried to observe the local customs and rituals.
I spoke the language better than most foreigners.
I was polite and unassuming.
I gave everyone the benefit of the doubt.
I went out of my way to make a good impression.

And still I was treated shabbily, laughed at, insulted. One day a sympathetic American friend who had been living there for years asked what I'd expected to find. "Greta Garbo and Melvyn Douglas in *Ninotchka*," I said. "That sparkling champagne ambience, that European *joie de vivre*, that carefree Gallic spirit."

He reminded me that *Ninotchka* was set in another time, a more innocent time, a time gone by. "Before the Nazi elite marched down the Champs-Élysées and moved into the Ritz for an indefinite stay."

According to him, the city hadn't recovered from World War II more than a decade later and still bore the scars of German occupation, Vichy's collaboration with the enemy, years of enforced curfews, rationing, hardships, all the while having to wait impotently for the Allied forces to restore its freedom and dignity.

"You're dealing with a castrated people," my friend said. "As Americans we remind them of their shame, defeat and dishonor.

They might like to pretend that to a man they were all fighting in the Resistance, but the truth is a lot of them were turning Jews and other 'undesirables' over to the Nazis. Of course they resent us."

His advice was that the next time a Frenchman acted obnoxious, I should return the favor. "Pretend you're a Nazi. Be arrogant. Treat him like dirt. It's the only thing that works."

It took me months to realize he was right and meanwhile I kept on dreaming abut the Paris of *Ninotchka*—smiling, carefree, amiable—and cursed my lousy timing. I moved to Paris in March 1959, soon after I married John Hultberg, a surrealist painter from Fresno, California. We had met in Provincetown the previous summer where John was managing an art gallery for Martha Jackson, the famous New York dealer, and I was attempting a reconciliation with my ex-husband whom I had divorced several years before. Why I ever imagined we could get back together considering our stormy past, is beyond me.

Nothing seemed to be going right that summer, not with my ex-husband and not with my second novel, *A Martini on the Other Table*, which I had just started. My first novel, *Getting Rid of Richard*, was in the hands of literary agent Sterling Lord whom I hoped would find a publisher for it before the summer ended. If he didn't—well, it was a possibility I tried not to think about. In the midst of all this anxiety, I met Hultberg. We were introduced by my friend, photographer Walter Silver, and it was love at first sight for both of us. *Un coup de foudre*, as the French would say. John was thirty-six, tall, blond, handsome, witty and talented. He'd won the Corcoran, the most prestigious art prize this country has to offer and his work had been featured in the pages of *Time* magazine. He was also an alcoholic, but since at first I never saw him drink anything except Coca-Cola I refused to believe he had a problem even though Walter and others tried to warn me.

Today I would probably be described as a co-dependent due to my affinity for men with a penchant for alcohol, but back then the syndrome was unheard of. It was only years later that I realized

I chose these men because they were drinking vicariously for me, my own alcoholism being in an inchoate stage. Despite our mutual attraction, it took a while before Hultberg and I got together—the entire summer in fact. Then just before Labor Day, we both wound up at an afternoon clambake where everyone was talking about what they planned to do when they returned to the city.

"How about you?" I asked John.

"I'm moving to Paris."

"With me, of course."

He didn't miss a beat. "Of course."

Even though it sounded like the idle banter of two strangers, I knew we weren't kidding. Within seconds a deal had been made, which we consummated in Hultberg's loft bed that same afternoon. Somehow my ex-husband got wind of this development and came barging in, drunk, wild-eyed, and barefoot. He had cut my only diaphragm in half and refused to leave unless I left with him, saying he was there to rescue me. I didn't want to be rescued. I was in love with Hultberg (two Johns in a row). Draping a blanket around myself, I descended the loft ladder and told him I was staying put.

"You've ruined my life, you bitch, but I'm not going anywhere without you," he declared.

"Yes, you are," Hultberg said, rushing to my aid. We had just discovered each other and the die was cast.

"Make me," Elbert taunted him.

Hultberg picked up a heavy bronze sculpture given to him by Mary Frank and threatened to hit him over the head with it unless he vacated the premises.

"Go ahead, do it." Elbert was grinning now, the sly cunning grin of the drunk. "You'll kill me and spend the rest of your life in prison."

Hultberg put down the sculpture and said he was in love with me. "Joyce and I are going to get married. I'm going to take care of her from now on."

This was the first I'd heard of it, but I couldn't have been more pleased. Aside from the fact that I had two good-looking men

101

fighting for my favors, which is always a big morale boost, I was impressed by John Hultberg. Unlike my ex-husband who kept threatening to write the great American novel and failed to write any novel at all, Hultberg was successful. His paintings were bought by knowledgeable connoisseurs, one was in the permanent collection of New York's Metropolitan Museum of Art, he had galleries in New York, Los Angeles, London, Milan and Paris. He lived on the Upper East Side, hobnobbed with Bill de Kooning and Franz Kline, went to snazzy gallery parties, was considered one of the most desirable bachelors in town and seemingly didn't have any financial problems.

I did. If Sterling Lord didn't sell *Getting Rid of Richard* by the end of the summer, it meant returning to my dump of an apartment on West 16th Street and my part-time secretarial job at Fairchild Publications for seventy-five dollars a week. Being a poor struggling writer at age twenty-eight was taking its toll and late at night I wondered if I would ever make a living with my writing. If not it meant working at secretarial jobs indefinitely, a dismal prospect. I had considered marrying for money, but didn't have the temperament to pull it off. I wasn't hard or calculating enough. I couldn't pretend to love someone I didn't love. It wasn't in my nature. What I needed was money *and* love. And now miraculously it had happened. I not only adored John Hultberg, I adored his gloomy paintings too. Executed in somber black, brown and gray tones, they revealed alien forbidding landscapes that didn't exist anywhere on earth, only in the tormented soul of their creator.

The first time I saw them in Martha Jackson's Provincetown gallery, I felt deeply moved and couldn't stop thinking about them. Apparently they also moved many other people who paid good money to hang them on their walls. Nobody had ever paid a cent for any of the plays that my ex-husband wrote, which made him cynical and angry. Although I sympathized with his plight, I knew that it had contributed to the breakup of our marriage. In America's competitive society, men were reared for success. They needed it, their egos thrived on it, withered without it and eventually their personal relationships withered too. Self-contempt killed these men's capacity for love and it was usually the wives who bore the brunt of their failure either through neglect, abuse or physical punishment. I had not been punished physically, only verbally, but so often and with so much barbed fury that in the end I couldn't take it any more. I felt sorry for women who remained locked in these destructive marriages. Thank God I had gotten out in time, I thought. Thank God for John Hultberg. He was just what the doctor ordered. Go and know.

When we returned to New York after our whirlwind romance, we decided not to rush into marriage but to live together for a while and see how it went. Having been divorced, too, John was as fearful as I of making another mistake. With some men I might have been apprehensive about such a casual arrangement, but I felt secure in John's love and convinced of its sincerity. He seemed to have eyes for no one except me and said he was happier than he had been in years.

"So am I," I truthfully replied.

New York looked beautiful that autumn, brimming with promise. We walked along the streets of the Upper East Side hand in hand, thrilled to be alive. Love made us smile and feel benign toward those less fortunate souls. *Love*. I had forgotten what an incredible sensation it was, how it turned the world upside down and made the most mundane things appear dazzling. Before long John found an apartment for us at the corner of 6th Street and Madison Avenue, right in the heart of the art gallery circuit. It was one flight up in a quaint old building, the ground floor still being used for commercial purposes. The apartment was a handsome floor-through with high ceilings and good light. John promptly claimed the front room and adjoining lavatory for his studio.

"That's where I was going to put my desk," I said, disappointed.

"I need the space more than you do. Why can't you write in the bedroom?"

I thought of Virginia Woolf's book, *A Room of One's Own*, and wondered if this was a harbinger of things to come. The bedroom had two doors, one of which led directly into John's studio, the other into our living room. "When I write, I'm locking the bedroom door," I told him. "If you want to get into the rest of the apartment, use your outside door and come around."

"What's the problem?"

"I don't like to be disturbed when I'm working. I'm sure you can understand that."

"Not really. It wouldn't bother me if you came in while I was painting. In fact I'd welcome the company."

"Well, I wouldn't so don't do it."

John's studio faced the prestigious Tibor de Nagy gallery across the street and our bedroom overlooked Madison Avenue's finest shops. It was a very expensive location. "Can you really afford this?" I asked my future husband. There was no question of my contributing anything toward the rent as we had agreed that I would quit my job in order to have more time for writing.

"I can afford most of it and Martha will make up the rest. She's going to store some of the gallery's paintings in our living room."

"How come?"

"She's strapped for space. It's a good idea, don't you think? We help her out and she helps us out."

I was hurt that he hadn't bothered to consult me. Given the choice, I would have preferred to live somewhere less posh and pay the entire rent ourselves, but since I wasn't paying rent maybe my wishes didn't count. It was an unsettling thought, making me wonder if it was a mistake to have quit my job. Accustomed to supporting myself, suddenly I felt like a non-person dependent upon the whims of John and Martha Jackson. I didn't like Martha and didn't trust her. The few times we met since our return from Provincetown, I saw that she regarded John as more than just another painter under contract to her gallery. Much more. She clearly adored him, worshipped him, gazed at him with big cow eyes, turned into a simpering teenager whenever she spoke to him.

The day after we moved into the 6th Street apartment, Martha marched in unannounced to inspect the premises, her gallery being only two blocks away. "We can put the racks over there," she said in an abnormally slow, sing-song voice that made people want to climb the walls. She pointed to the far end of the living room where I had planned to build bookshelves. "I'll send someone by tomorrow to install them." Then she smiled an insincere smile and said she hoped I would be happy in my new home.

"I'd be happy wherever John was."

"Who wouldn't?" she replied, not bothering to disguise her infatuation.

"That woman is in love with you," I told John after she left. "She can't take her eyes off you. There's something more going on here than the usual painter-dealer relationship. Did you have an affair with her?"

"It wasn't an affair," he said, uneasily. "We had too much to drink one night and fell into bed. It was a long time ago. It didn't mean anything."

"Maybe not to you. It sure meant something to Martha."

"That's ridiculous. She thinks of me as a son."

"She should. She's old enough to be your mother." I refrained from adding that Martha was one of the most devious and hostile people I had ever met. "I dislike the idea of relying on her financially."

"Why? She has money to burn. She's a Kellogg from Buffalo and was a millionaire even before she started the gallery."

"So what? You're still beholden to her. Doesn't that bother you?"

"Not for a minute," my future husband said.

The Martha Jackson Gallery, located in her elegant four-story townhouse on East 69th Street between Madison and Park, was internationally acclaimed. Her artists were bold, talented, innovative. Their paintings and sculptures commanded top prices. Martha's gala openings were events not to be missed. Everyone in the art world came and more often than not, Martha herself was the star attraction, people gravitating toward her because she wielded

105

so much power. They flattered her shamelessly, sat still for her sly insults, turned red when she looked straight through them as though they hadn't just given her a warm "hello."

Mark Rothko grabbed Hultberg at one of these events, bewildered. "What did I do? She won't talk to me. Have I offended her in some way?"

It turned out that Martha had mistaken him for a cook she'd fired. "Oh Mark, you look just like that awful Vittorio," I heard her say later in that grating voice. "He burned the risotto the night David Smith came to dinner. It was inedible."

The only two people who didn't seem put off by her were Louise Nevelson (whom Martha represented) and Larry Rivers (whom she didn't). One evening at a Tibor de Nagy opening, I ran into Larry whom I'd known since I was eight years old, his younger sister having been my best friend. I asked him why he and Louise were immune to Martha's brand of intimidation.

"Louise and I come from a long line of Russian peasants," he said. "Our parents fled the old country in order to escape the pogroms. After the Cossacks, who'd be afraid of Martha Jackson?"

I found it hard to believe that anyone who appeared as semi-retarded as Martha could be responsible for having created such a classy sophisticated gallery and asked John for an explanation.

"She has a rare talent for picking artists who are going to become famous," he said. "I can't figure out how she does it and neither can anyone else because in practically every other area, she's a moron."

I loved his answer and since I loved him, I decided not to let Martha Jackson ruin my happiness. Still I knew that we would be much better off if we didn't live so close to her gallery-cum-residence, one disadvantage being that she considered us captive audiences for her frequent dinner parties, to which she invited the art world's most select people. John's reluctance to attend these affairs made him edgy and ill-humored even before we left our apartment and once there he buried his head in a book, ignoring the other guests.

"If you're so miserable about going, why do you continue to do it?" I asked.

"It's a command performance."

"What does that mean exactly?"

"It means I have to go."

Martha didn't have a clue as to what constituted good food and had hired an incompetent cook named Horace to preside in the kitchen. A thwarted opera singer, Horace's culinary repertoire was limited to indigestible southern dishes. God knows where she found him. She treated Horace as abominably as she did everyone in her employ while at the same time languishing a great deal of affection on her newest acquisition, a parrot coincidentally named Horace. The parrot's usual perch was on Martha's shoulder, except during mealtimes when he was exiled to the living room. Martha had taught him one sentence, which he repeated with shrill and boring fidelity. "ABSTRACT EXPRESSIONISM IS HERE TO STAY."

At these soirées Martha sat at the head of a handsome rosewood table, commanding in a deceptively simple black dress set off by exotic jewelry. Her china, crystal and silver were the very best, as was the vintage wine recommended by her French art adviser, Michel Tapie. Although the food ranged from mediocre to terrible, Martha was oblivious. If she felt it necessary to call Horace (the cook) into the room, she tapped on her wine glass with a dessert fork. Unfortunately she had a habit of tapping whenever he was engaged in some delicate kitchen operation, causing him to ignore her summons. This made her tap even louder. Still no sign of the cook. Throwing etiquette to the winds, she would shout, "Horace, come in here immediately!" The result was instant collision between the angry black man and the jungle-green parrot babbling, "ABSTRACT EXPRESSIONISM IS HERE TO STAY." Guests used to choke laughing on their black-eyed peas, much to Martha's confusion since she didn't see anything funny in the situation.

"She has no sense of humor," I said to John after the first such incident had occurred.

"No, absolutely none at all."

Since humor was one of the strongest bonds between John and me, later I wondered if it had blinded me to serious problems in the relationship. One problem was his stinginess and another, I soon realized, was his drinking. I had never run across this particular combination in the same person, since all the drinkers I knew tended to be free and easy with a buck. While John thought nothing of dropping fifty dollars at the Cedar Tavern for the privilege of getting smashed and insulting Franz Kline, he was a skinflint when it came to ordinary expenditures.

For instance we never bought clothing, never entertained, made do with only the most essential pieces of furniture and never exchanged gifts. He also refused to let me have my own checking account in order to pay the local tradesmen. This meant that every time a delivery boy appeared on our doorstep (and we lived in a neighborhood where all the stores delivered), I had to ask John for the money. It was not only inconvenient, it was humiliating, but I hoped that in time he would loosen up. He didn't. Now I realize that there are three areas in which people's habits are the most rigid and inflexible—sex, food and money.

Far worse than the money problem, however, were his cyclic drinking bouts. Even though he abstained from alcohol most of the time, whenever he decided to go out and have "a drink" it turned into a bender that lasted anywhere from twelve to twenty-four hours and culminated in his staying in bed for the next two days, recovering. This pattern seemed to take place once a month with eerie regularity, meaning that for three and a half weeks I was dealing with a sane sober person and for half a week I had a maniac on my hands. One morning when he rolled in still plastered, his tan gabardine suit looked as though it had spent the night on Skid Row. John himself was white and shaky. "I tried to jump in front of a moving car, but a Greek sculptor dragged me back," he said. "I thought he was attacking me, so I punched him and we rolled around in the gutter before I realized he saved my life."

"Do me a favor," I said. "The next time you decide to get plastered, wear a dark suit. The man at the dry cleaners told me never to bring that tan suit of yours in again. It seems the stains are beyond them."

"What stains?"

Heavy going as much of this was, it comprised only part of our relationship and from my jaundiced point of view, a small part at that. Mostly I felt happy with John, secure, protected, loved, and mentally stimulated. He opened up a whole new world of art to me, one that I had never explored before. Just walking down the street with him was a revelatory experience because of the visual details he noticed along the way. We approached everything from two different angles. Mine was through words, his through images. He changed my life forever, forcing me to open my eyes.

What we had in common was that we were both workaholics. At last I had found a man who wanted the same kind of life I did. John not only understood my compulsion to write (his compulsion to paint being even more pronounced), he made it possible for me to do so under very pleasant conditions. With no office to report to, there were no jangling alarm clocks in the morning, no packed subway trains, no energy-sapping labor that all of my mundane jobs had entailed. It was like being let out of prison. I tried not to think about my first novel, *Getting Rid of Richard*, which Sterling Lord was still submitting to publishers but to concentrate on the new one in my typewriter, *A Martini on the Other Table*. Then one afternoon, Sterling called to say that Putnam was interested in publishing *Richard* providing they could find a softcover house to do the reprint.

"Since you're an unknown quantity, Putnam has to protect themselves financially," Sterling explained. "I'll keep you posted."

G.P. Putnam & Sons had an excellent reputation for fiction, as did their editor, Bob Amussen, who recommended that they buy the book. My professional future suddenly looked promising and every night I prayed for the two-way deal to be consummated. Meanwhile my days began to fall into a predictable pattern. Being early risers, John and I spent the morning working, he on his paintings and I on my book. Compared to the first one, which had been relatively trouble-free, *A Martini on the Other Table* was fraught with hurdles right from the start and reminded me of the truism about second books being the hardest to write. After lunch we usually dropped by the gallery to see if Martha had sold any of John's paintings. While there was still considerable interest in his work, overall sales figures had dropped since the advent of abstract expressionism. Many painters knowing a fast buck when they saw it, jumped on the abstract expressionist bandwagon literally overnight. John refused to do so and went on working in his usual surrealist style, even though it cost him a lot of money to stick to his principles.

When the weather was nice, we took long walks in the afternoon stopping off at galleries and museums. Wherever we went, John knew people—interesting people, creative people, famous people. There was much handshaking and backslapping, inquiries about upcoming exhibits, gossip about dealers, curators, and other artists. Our evenings were up for grabs. Sometimes we stayed home and worked a second shift, sometimes we went to art openings at landmark galleries, to dinner parties at the homes of wealthy European collectors, to loft parties that had pulsating music, free-flowing liquor, colorfully-attired painters and sculptors.

"*Do you paint, too?*"

If I was asked that question once, I was asked it fifty times and not in a very friendly manner. When I said I didn't, the inquisitor lost interest in anything else I might have to say, the general attitude being that if I wasn't part of the cliquish New York art world I might as well not exist. Certain people were downright insulting. At the stylish Staemphli gallery, a well known collagist took me aside. "So you're the clever little girl who snared our most desirable bachelor," she said, giving me a withering look. "Frankly I can't imagine what he sees in you."

I was too dumbstruck to reply. When I told John about these encounters, he said that as soon as I got a book published I would be treated with more respect.

"Why can't they treat me with more respect now? Who do they think they are?"

"They're confused because you're not like most painters' wives. You're not the earth mother type or the dumb blonde type, both of whom live exclusively for their genius of a husband. You have an identity of your own, a career of your own, opinions that differ from mine. I love you for it, but it puts these people off. Basically they're a bunch of sheep."

While it was a flattering explanation, it didn't help alleviate the pain I felt whenever I was rudely dismissed yet one more time. Sometimes after being asked if I were a painter, I would say, "No, a writer."

Barest flicker of interest. "What have you had published?"

"Nothing."

Flicker of interest dies, but completely. Instead of wondering what the future held for me in such a rigid, small-minded world, I wondered if my problems wouldn't be solved by our moving to Paris. I hadn't been able to get that city out of my mind and finally asked John why he had abandoned our original plans.

"They're not abandoned," he said.

"Merely postponed."

"Until when?"

"That depends."

"On what?"

"A lot of things." And he changed the subject.

I didn't know what to think. Was he stalling? Lying? Had Paris been some kind of fantasy? Just as I was about to give up hope of ever living there, John came home one afternoon after a rushed trip to Martha's and said we were going. "Martha has arranged for me to have a show in Paris and also Milan." He was very excited. "We'll sublet this apartment and rent one on the Left Bank. A lot of American painters have moved over there. It will be fun."

If a lot of American painters had moved over, why would things be any easier for me than in New York? Did I ask myself that question? Of course not. I was too bitten by the travel bug to be logical. "When do we leave?"

"As soon as I paint forty pictures. Starting immediately, turn down all invitations for the next two months. I'll be holed up in my studio night and day."

He wasn't kidding. I barely saw him after that, except at mealtimes. One evening when we were having dinner, I said, "Since we're going to be living abroad, don't you think we should get married? Wouldn't it be more practical?"

John was happily surprised. "You mean you want to marry me now that you know how crazy I am?"

"You're not crazy, you're eccentric. And of course I want to marry you, I'm in love with you."

"Hey, this is swell!" He pulled me off the chair and we began to dance around the living room with a lot of thudding energy. The polka, the only dance he knew.

"I'm getting married in the morning!" he sang.

My closest friends, Libby and Walter Silver, had just been married at City Hall and when we decided to follow their lead, they agreed to be our witnesses. Then Sterling called to say that the editors at Fawcett were enthusiastic about reprinting *Getting Rid of Richard* in softcover, providing they could reach a mutually satisfactory agreement with Putnam. I couldn't believe that so many auspicious things were happening all at once and wondered if it was a smart idea to leave the country in case Putnam or Fawcett wanted me to do revisions, but the thought was so disconcerting that I pushed it out of my mind.

On the day of my wedding, Libby told me that she and Walter, a freelance photojournalist, had decided to move to Paris, too. I couldn't have been happier as both of them were supportive of me in my continuing battle with the hostile art world. When the time came to tie the knot, John was amused that I had chosen to be married in a slinky black satin Suzy Wong type dress, with deep slits up both sides. I was amused that the civil servant who performed the ceremony mispronounced both our last names. Afterward we took the ferry to Hoboken for a half-day celebration, then it was back home and back to the studio for John to continue amassing those forty paintings.

Martha acknowledged our wedding announcement with a chilly "congratulations" and never mentioned it again or gave us a present, which I guess I deserved since I hadn't invited her to the nuptials. Her attitude toward me changed from indifference to icy coldness, but I was too busy with packing arrangements to care and before I knew it the big day had arrived. At the beginning of March 1959 we sailed for Le Havre on the *Liberté*, one of the last great ocean-going liners. Martha came to the farewell party in our stateroom, which although officially classified as cabin class boasted both a porthole and enough space to qualify for first-class. It was a sumptuous accommodation and I doubted if John had the money or the inclination to have paid for it.

The stateroom was packed with friends and well-wishers who were drinking champagne and asking if they would ever see us again. Having sublet our 6th Street apartment to Martha's son and daughter-in-law, we told everyone we were going to live in Paris forever. Painters Paul Jenkins and Alice Baber were also sailing on the *Liberté*, but in third-class since Paul hadn't yet become the huge success he would be in later years.

"This is a fantastic cabin," I said to John during the ongoing tumult. "How did you swing it?"

"Martha's office made all the arrangements. They're good at things like that."

I almost asked if Martha's office had also picked up the tab, but part of me didn't want to know. The five-day crossing was rough with stormy, windy, rainy weather that rendered me violently seasick for the entire voyage, the worst moments being at mealtimes when the floor of the huge dining room pitched and swayed in the storm. Unlike me, John relished the inclement weather and went for long brisk walks on the deck, rain slashing him in the face, a true Viking.

On a more positive note, I loved that all the signs on board were in French, the crew and staff were bilingual, menus were not only printed in French with no translation provided, they offered dishes I had never heard of. I figured it was a good way to start learning what I would need to know once we got to Paris. To say that I was nervous about fitting in was putting it mildly. Even though I had studied the language for nearly five years in school, I was afraid I wouldn't be able to speak it with the proper accent. I was afraid of making a fool of myself in the most sophisticated city in Europe.

From Le Havre we took the boat train to Paris. At mid-morning, the conductor knocked on our compartment door and asked John if he wished to make a luncheon reservation, whereupon there followed a fast exchange about which service we desired and some other details. "I can't believe it," I said after the conductor had left. "You were speaking French and I understood every word."

John regarded me with surprise. "You're not nervous about living in Paris, are you?"

"Well, maybe a little."

It was dark when we arrived and I will never forget how stunning Paris looked, lit up and sparkling, pure magic. No movie or travel poster could capture the beauty that lay stretched out in front of me: symmetrical, orderly, measured, different from anything I was used to, the buildings were so low that I felt I could see the city in its entirety. There were trees everywhere, there was room to breathe and a sense that unlike New York, which was devoted to making money, Paris was devoted to pleasure. I felt like pinching myself. I was actually in the City of Light, the fashion capital of the world, the *sina qua non* of international chic.

"What do you think?" John asked.

"I'm overwhelmed."

John had lived in Paris before, knew his way around, knew what to expect. By the time we checked into the Hotel du Quai Voltaire overlooking the Seine, my awe of the city now included my awe of its people. I had never seen anything like them. With only a modicum of innate good looks, they managed to transform themselves into swaggering works of art. I wondered how they did it, by what conjurer's trick, and they all did it. The homeliest man projected an air of suave Continental élan, while the plainest woman carried herself like a movie star. No detail of her outfit or makeup had been neglected, no attempt to gild the lily had been ignored, and yet the touch was so subtle that it never approached vulgarity. I applauded this triumph of artifice even as I felt utterly intimidated by it.

"My clothes are all wrong," I moaned when we were unpacking. "My hairstyle is dated. My shoes are dowdy. My makeup sucks. And my lack of sophistication sticks out a mile."

"You're imagining it," John said, giving me a reassuring hug.

But I wasn't, at least not by Parisian standards which suddenly were the only ones that mattered, all of my New York confidence having gone up in smoke. I wanted to look as bold as the women I had seen, I wanted to look as alluring and self-assured even though I suspected their achievement had less to do with expensive clothing and more with some centuries-old secret that American women weren't privy to. By comparison we were a far more androgynous group, timid about playing up our female attributes to the fullest, whereas the French didn't suffer from such puritanical considerations.

"Let's go to the Deux Magots for a drink," John said after we had put everything away.

My desire to see the café made famous by the existentialist writers overcame my desire to crawl into bed and pull the covers over my head, so I fixed my lipstick and ran a comb through my badly-cut hair (which had looked fine in New York). "I'm ready to face the music," I said as we left the hotel and began walking toward the Boulevard St. Germain. The more we walked and the more Parisian chic I saw, the more I realized that anxious times had just begun.

"We have to do two things," John said the next morning over brioches and café au lait. "Check in with my gallery dealer and find an apartment. In that order."

The Gallerie du Dragon, located on the nearby rue du Dragon, was a small avant-garde establishment with a growing reputation. It was run by a young good-looking Basque named Max Clerac-Serou and his South American girlfriend, Cecilia. They were an attractive couple currently featuring a show of the Italian surrealist, Matta. John's show would be next and although he had brought some canvases with him from New York, the bulk was still to be shipped by Martha. She had told us she was sending his best paintings to Paris and the worst to Milan, since the influential art critics were in Paris while the buyers, who had the money but no taste, were in Milan. After John and Max finished discussing business, we mentioned our housing problem.

"You're going to have a hard time finding anything reasonable," Max said. "A very hard time, I'm afraid."

He was right. Parisians didn't move as frequently or whimsically as New Yorkers, far from it. Rentals were non-existent except in the exorbitant price range, and those who owned their flats seemed to give them up only when they died. After a fruitless search, we realized that our best hope was for an eventual sublet and in the meantime Max suggested that we wait it out at the Hotel Taranne, which was situated directly above the famous Brasserie Lipp, on Boulevard St. Germain.

This struck us as a good idea since the Tarrane was conveniently located and much less expensive than the Quai Voltaire, which catered to transients. Besides, I had heard that my hero, Albert Camus (the Algerian Humphrey Bogart) frequently dined at Lipp and I hoped to catch a glimpse of him. The Hotel Tarrane boasted a primarily French clientele, many of its residents having been there for years. Living in hotels was an accepted Parisian custom, particularly among single people who wanted to avoid housekeeping chores and take their meals out. I had gleaned that much from reading Simone de Beauvoir's first novel, *She Came to Stay*, in which her hero and heroine kept permanent rooms at just such a hotel even though they could have easily afforded a nice apartment.

It didn't take me long to understand the desire to eat out. Food in Paris was sublime, not only at expensive restaurants but even at the most insignificant café and contrary to the rich sauces and complicated dishes I had expected, it was for the most part very simple fare. That confused me no end. How did they turn a lamb chop or a dish of string beans into such a delectable feast? I felt compelled to unearth their culinary secrets even if it meant wending my way through the kitchens of Paris from the Left Bank to the Right. For someone who had never been compulsive about food or worried about her weight, I was about to embark on the eating binge of all time.

"You are the only Americans staying here."

The woman who manned the front desk at the Hotel Tarrane eyed our passports suspiciously, making it clear she wished we had gone elsewhere. Still she gave us a nice big airy room. It overlooked the busy Boulevard St. Germain and from its window we had an unobstructed view of the Deux Magots as well as a neighboring café, the Flore, another well-known existentialist hangout. The room's furnishings consisted of a double bed, an old-fashioned armoire, two chairs with faded seat cushions, a worn but decent carpet, and a desk where I could write. The bathroom had a tub, sink, and bidet. The W.C. was across the hall. I had never before seen a bidet and couldn't imagine one existing in a modest American hotel any more than I could imagine a gleaming shower stall in the Tarrane.

Our weekly tariff included a Continental breakfast. When we were ready to order it, all we had to do was reach for the wall phone above the bed, call downstairs, and say we would like to have it sent up. The first morning there I discovered John had a problem doing that. "I can't make the phone call," he admitted.

"What do you mean? Why not?"

"I would start laughing hysterically the minute I opened my mouth."

"I don't understand."

"Neither do I, but that's the way it is. There's something else. I can't be anywhere in sight when the waitress arrives with our breakfast."

"Where will you be?"

"In the bathroom or the closet, but if there isn't enough time to reach either of those two places I'll dive under the bed." He added. "Don't be alarmed."

One morning our waitress who came in with only a muffled knock, happened to notice a pair of striped pajamas sticking out from under the bed. When she turned to me for an explanation, I said my husband was eccentric—in French, of course, even though I had to look the word up in my Larousse. Nobody at the Taranne spoke a word of English. After that to spare John the agony of having to make the breakfast call, I made it myself and soon had it down to a pat formula. *Bonjour, Madame. Deux petits dejeuner, s'il vous plait. Merci, Madame.*

Then one morning I urged him to try it thinking I could affect a cure. Lots of luck. He began laughing hysterically the second he began talking into the receiver and any attempt to control himself only made the words come out in even more staccato bursts of hilarity, followed by no apology or explanation, just a slamming down of the receiver after which he raced into the closet, his quota of anxiety thoroughly exhausted. The woman at the front desk began to give him incriminating looks and no wonder. She clearly thought he was nuts. When I started writing in the morning, wearing a raincoat over my nightgown (I didn't own a robe and John refused to give me the money to buy one), she included me in her dark stare.

Aside from our daily breakfast trauma, living at the Tarrane was a pleasant experience and I couldn't wait for Walter and Libby to get there. They were not only my closest friends, they had a great sense of humor and I was dying to fill them in on all that had transpired since we last saw each other in New York. When they arrived, they were luckier than we were in finding a place of their own. Within days they had moved into a tiny but charming two-story house not far from the Tarrane. The only convenience it lacked was a refrigerator, but Libby seemed undaunted and said that very few Parisians owned one.

"Aren't you afraid of food getting spoiled?" I asked her.

"No, I'll go to the market every day just like the French housewives. Everything they serve is fresher than fresh."

"Maybe that's the secret of the food in restaurants. Freshness. I've never tasted anything like it."

"Neither have I. I'm beginning to feel quite gluttonous. I hope I don't get fat."

"You?" Libby was a rail. "I'm the one who should be worried. I can't wait for my next meal."

John knew a lot of people in Paris, all of them involved in the art world in one way or another. Walter and Libby fit neatly into this tight little circle, Walter having been the unofficial photographer for many artists of the New York School before they became successful. During their struggling years they used to give Walter a painting in exchange for a photograph usually needed for a catalogue. As a result, Walter had amassed an impressive collection and ruefully liked to tell about the day he photographed Jackson Pollack and then turned down one of his oils because it was raining and he didn't want it to get wet. With Pollack's death soon afterward, the oil would have been worth a staggering amount of money or as my husband was fond of saying, "If you're an artist, it pays to die. Look what happened to that poor bastard, Van Gogh."

I now found myself caught up in an even livelier social life than back in New York where getting together with friends happened mostly indoors. In Paris, it was just the opposite. The French loved to take turns sitting at outdoor cafés watching each other strut by. They were a very visual race, whether appreciating a Rodin sculpture or the curve of a woman's hip. After centuries of practice, their aesthetic eye had become precise and measured. I still remember the day that Libby and I went to a Right Bank department store because she wanted to buy pair of gray gloves. We were stunned when the saleswoman pulled open a drawer to reveal not two, not four, not even seven, but thirteen shades of gray gloves lined up in deepening intensity. "Which shade would suit Madame best?" she inquired.

With no studio of his own, John had found a communal atelier where he could make lithographs, a process that was new to him and which he seemed to enjoy. I spent the morning working on my novel and finishing off the generous double portions of bread, butter and preserves from our Continental breakfast. Then in the early afternoon I bathed, dressed, and went to meet my husband at a nearby café. After spending so many hours at the typewriter, I welcomed the mindless distraction of art world news and gossip. In the evening we crossed paths with many of the same people at the Coupole, the Dome, and the Deux Magots. There were also dinner parties that went on late into the night with good food and wine. These were lively affairs because for the first time in history American painters had stolen the spotlight from their French colleagues and it was a heady sensation to be part of that high-flying group.

One cloud marred my good mood. Here as in New York, I was repeatedly asked if I painted too. When I said I didn't, the rejection was more polite but it hurt nonetheless. Except for Walter and Libby, nobody thought much of me and made no attempt to hide it. John was the star in the family, I was merely the wife. It rankled, but I kept my spirits up by hoping that Putnam and Fawcett would come to an understanding and publish *Getting Rid of Richard*. Being surrounded by successful people, day in and day out, was taking its toll. I asked Libby, an aspiring writer herself, how she dealt with it.

"It doesn't affect me at all," she said. "Walter hasn't achieved John's exalted status, so nobody pays any attention to us. Either of us."

"Doesn't that bother you? The reason why they don't? The snobbism?"

"I guess it would if I weren't so impressed by their accomplishments. Also you have to admit they're a lot of fun to be around most of the time."

"You mean when they're not busy acting as though nothing in the world matters except achieving fame as a painter or sculptor?"

"For these people, nothing does."

Much as I admired her laid-back attitude, I knew I would never be able to emulate it. I was more ambitious than Libby.

The day before John's exhibition was due to open at the Gallerie du Dragon, Matta's paintings were taken down and John's were put up. He helped Max Clerac-Serou with the arrangements, all the while mumbling disparaging remarks about his own work. As each painting was hung, he saw its faults and wanted to grab a brush to correct them. No amount of reassurance from any of us lessened his discontent. Afterward he said that most painters were never satisfied with what they had created and if left to their own devices, would repaint ad infinitum.

"My teacher at the Art Student's League tried to nip this tendency in the bud," he added. "His advice was, 'Stop before you improve it.'"

There was a big turnout at the gallery the following evening. Not only all our friends but half of Paris showed up, with the crowd spilling over onto the sidewalk to drink the wine and eat the hors d'ouevres provided by Max and Cecilia. Walter was busy taking pictures of the event. A few red stars began to appear alongside some of John's paintings, not as many as we hoped for but enough to make the show a respectable financial success. Reviews would come later. As much as we wanted to stay up late and celebrate with the others, we had to catch a train for Milan early the next morning so as to be on hand for John's second exhibition within twenty-four hours. After Milan, we planned to spend some vacation time in Venice and Rome.

"You lucky girl, you," Walter said, kissing me goodbye. "Not everyone gets a free tour of Italia."

"Nothing is free, Walter."

John's show in Milan was underway by the time we walked in to find more than a few red stars mounted alongside some of his more expensively-priced paintings. I could see what Martha meant by sending the worst ones here because compared to the show in Paris, these canvases were second-rate. If John was embarrassed by them, he didn't say anything. The gallery was large, modern, gleaming, and owned by a chic young comtessa who had drawn a crowd that was much more fashionable and wealthy than the crowd in Paris and didn't mind flaunting it. The women wore designer dresses, good jewelry, and appeared to have just come from the hairdresser's. The men were just as smartly attired with that swaggering Italian flair no American man could copy. Not only did I feel wrinkled and grubby after the long train ride, but when I learned that we were invited to a dinner party being given in our honor immediately afterward, I realized I'd have no time to shower or change.

"How can I go anywhere in this dress?" I said, referring to the swirling green and black challis print I had hastily put on that morning in Paris. Having bought no clothes since my marriage, there was little to choose from. "It makes me look like I'm on secret army maneuvers in the Philippine jungles."

John, who had no sartorial sense and wore strangely cut gabardine suits reminiscent of another time, was unsympathetic. "You're a writer. You're a painter's wife. You're not expected to be glamorous. You look fine. Stop worrying so much."

I looked horrible and worried even more when the comtessa said that the dinner party was being given by a Milanese socialite and her Swedish husband who just happened to be dentist to the Pope. They had bought several of John's paintings and were anxious to meet the artist. As we approached our destination, the neighborhood began to change from respectable to ultra-exclusive and I noticed that John's suit had attracted a few stains since we'd started out that morning. (Was this the same suit that the Madison Avenue dry cleaner refused to ever work on again?)

Our hosts' home was nothing short of spectacular. Done in marble, glass and pale wood, it contained rare tapestries, valuable modern artwork and 17th-century antiques. The opulence continued into the powder room where all the fittings were of solid gold and lapis lazuli. With the sense that I had mistakenly wandered onto an Antonioni movie set, I returned to the others who by now were seated around a circular dining table for eight. A small roly-poly man was introduced to me as the Spaghetti King of Bologna. He spoke no English and since I spoke no Italian, he plaintively asked me in French if I didn't think Damon Runyon was the greatest American writer who ever lived. I can't remember my answer because I was too busy wishing the floor would swallow me up. Compared to the three other women who were exquisitely gowned, coiffed and bejeweled, I looked like a match girl. John didn't fare much better in his stained suit and scuffed shoes. The difference was that either he didn't realize it or he didn't care.

I was seated to the right of my host, the Swedish haute dentist who happened to be an extremely handsome chunk of Nordic charm. As a white-gloved butler served dish after dish of beautifully-prepared food, my host regaled me with stories of his days in Hollywood when he capped the teeth of movie stars. "No actor wants to be responsible for holding up production just because one of his caps has broken," he confided. "So I always kept a duplicate set in my office, in case of an emergency."

"Who was your most famous patient?"

"Marilyn Monroe. She was also the most difficult to anaesthetize. For a lovely sensitive woman, she had the constitution of an ox."

I was only half-listening, being too distracted by the sight of my husband on the other side of the table throwing back the vino with furious abandon. I could see that he was angry at these people who having paid for his company in cold hard cash, were now pretending to treat him as a social equal while actually considering themselves his patrons, and hence his superiors. I knew that to John it was he, the artist, the visionary, the creative force who was superior, yet protocol wouldn't permit him to say so. The more he drank, the more stiff and haughty his demeanor became, the more acid his remarks, the more he seemed to physically detach himself from these well-heeled philistines.

I watched his gallery dealer, the young comtessa, try to dissuade him from taking another glass of wine, but in vain. He was hell-bent on numbing himself into oblivion. Once the meal was blessedly over, John stood up, swayed, and staggered into the living room where coffee and brandy were being served. Two of the Milanese matrons, aglow in diamonds and rubies, exchanged a smug look behind his back. "This is no way to behave," I whispered in his ear.

"Why not?" he sneered. "Aren't I supposed to be the jolly court jester?"

"You're not jolly, you're drunk. Please don't have anything more to drink."

He paid no attention to me and passed out cold on the sofa a little while later. Our host and the Spaghetti King of Bologna put him in a taxi, smiling at me sympathetically. So much for *la dolce vita*. By comparison, Venice was restful and serene. I loved being on the water again and since it was off-season, there were hardly any tourists to clog the charming narrow cobblestoned streets. We didn't know a soul for a change and spent a quiet week relaxing, my only disappointment being that John refused to hire a gondola saying it was too expensive.

"Am I destined to be the only woman who goes to Venice and doesn't get to ride in a gondola?" I asked.

"Looks like it," he said.

Rome, on the other hand, was noisy, bustling and filled with familiar faces. We ran around with Conrad Marca-Relli, Scarpitta, Marisol, Alberto Burri, Patsy and Mike Goldberg. It was like Paris all over again in that we were forever meeting friends at cafés during the day and then meeting them again in the evening at popular trattorias for late dinners. Although it was fun, I was getting tired of eating all our meals out and equally tired of hotel rooms. I longed for a place of our own, the pleasure of preparing a home-cooked meal, solitude. One day at the American Express office, I found a letter from Sterling saying Fawcett wanted me to do revisions on *Getting*

Rid of Richard before they'd agree to reprint it. He had sent Fawcett's letter to our Paris address and asked that I contact him after I read it.

"Maybe this will be your big break," John said.

"Let's hope." I wondered what kind of revisions Fawcett had in mind. When we returned to Paris, the chestnut trees were in bloom and the cafés had removed their glassed-in enclosures. Gone were the heavy overcoats and thick sweaters of winter, replaced by lighter brighter clothing. Spring had arrived at last, bringing with it two pieces of news, one good, one bad. The bad news was that after reading Fawcett's letter, I realized I disagreed with all of their suggestions for "improving" my novel. Even worse, I couldn't decide what to do about it. Should I fly back to New York and discuss it with their editors? Should I flatly turn them down? Should I put aside my personal misgivings and bow to their professional expertise? I made the mistake of choosing the last course of action.

The good news was that an apartment had become available, a duplex. The painter who owned it was leaving for an extended stay in America and would agree to a long-term sublet, which was what we wanted. What we didn't want was to have to move out of our arrondissement, so it came as jolt to learn that the apartment was in Montparnasse. Still we made an appointment to see it.

"Montparnasse depresses me," I told John as we walked over. "It's too far from the Seine."

"Yes, but we would be right off Boulevard Raspail, which is a great location. The Dome and Coupole are practically around the corner."

I'm a staunch believer in symbols and the minute the building came into view, I knew it would be disastrous to live there because it overlooked the Montparnasse cemetery. Our apartment was on the fifth floor with windows facing front, which meant the first sight to greet us each morning would be a solid block of gravestones. However even I had to admit that the apartment itself was charming and suitable to our needs. The living room was large enough for John to set up an easel at one end and for me to write on a long trestle table at the other end. The kitchen had a fridge—I couldn't wait to tell Libby—and a fairly modern range-oven. Upstairs was a cozy bedroom-bathroom suite.

"The price is right," John said. "And Simone de Beauvoir lives on the ground floor."

He knew I would be impressed by that since I had just read *The Second Sex*, a feminist book that was years ahead of its time and had knocked me for a loop. My admiration for Mme. de Beauvoir was boundless and if she thought it was okay to live opposite a cemetery, maybe I was overreacting. (Only later did I realize that from her ground-floor vantage point, she couldn't see the tombstones because of a high railing.) We arranged to sublet the apartment but since it wouldn't be ready for a few weeks, we accepted a friend's offer to share his home in Montmartre rather than go back to our room at the Tarrane.

John told me that Hemi Fara, a sophisticated and debonair Egyptian, was known as the secret art dealer of Paris because certain pieces in his valuable collection were reputedly acquired by devious means and also because they had a way of disappearing every so often, only to be replaced by other pieces of equal value. When asked what had happened to the missing artwork, Hemi would shrug and smile enigmatically. In short, he managed to live quite well without pursing any obvious occupation. Henri loved cats and his female had just given birth to a litter that was being housed in a gazebo at the far end of the garden. Over the next few weeks I became attached to two of the kittens, a gray male and a black female. When the time came for us to move to Montparnasse, Henri gave them to me as a housewarming gift. I named the female "Radis" and the male "Beurre" in honor of my favorite French appetizer, radishes with butter.

"I will miss *mes petits choux*," Henri declared, giving the kittens a passionate goodbye kiss. "Make sure they get plenty of milk. They've barely been weaned."

Later I learned that I had saved the kittens from a sure death as every time Henri's female had a litter, he would wring all their necks or as someone remarked, "Sentimentality and cruelty often go hand in hand."

The weeks that followed were busy ones. What with setting up housekeeping on rue Schelscher, acclimating myself to a new neighborhood, and doing revisions for Fawcett (wondering if I had made the right decision), I had my hands full. As soon as I mailed the revisions to Sterling, I put my literary anxieties on the back burner and plunged into domesticity full-force. After so many months of hotel living, I couldn't wait to start cooking again, but I soon discovered that instead of supermarkets, Montparnasse had a variety of specialized shops, none of which delivered and all of which were closed for three hours in the middle of the day.

In order to buy several disparate items such as a couple of lamb chops, a chunk of cheese, and half a kilo of tomatoes, I had to patronize three different establishments and stand on three different lines. (Nothing in the area was self-service.) Often these lines were long and slow-moving because of the French tendency to haggle over every detail. I tried to get used to the endless delays by reminding myself that the food tasted better than anything found in American supermarkets, still it was an extremely frustrating and time-consuming process.

There was the bakery, the fishmonger, the veggie and fruit stalls, the cheese shop, and so on. Even the butcher didn't sell poultry. For that I had to go shlepping down the street to the poultry man who killed, plucked, cleaned and trussed the chickens in back of his store while you waited. The butcher didn't sell horse meat either (assuming you wanted it). Only the horse meat butcher sold that. What this boiled down to was an incredible amount of time spent dragging groceries back from the market. One trip in the morning was rarely enough and I began to feel like a beast of burden when I had to return later that afternoon. With three big milk drinkers at home (John and the two cats), milk was a steady item on my list, but it didn't come in cardboard containers—only in glass bottles that weighed a ton. When I realized that three bottles were all I could carry in my quaint string shopping bag (no store provided paper bags), I started to despair.

In New York, the Gristede's on Madison Avenue accepted phoned-in grocery orders, which were then rushed to our door by a polite delivery boy, so that if I didn't feel like it I didn't even have to leave our apartment in order to get everything I needed. I was spoiled, no question of it, and yet if Gristede's had been the height of convenience, the markets in Montparnasse were the pits. "Even though we eat out several nights a week, the amount of time I spend shopping is ridiculous," I told John. "It's driving me crazy and I don't know what to do about it."

"I suppose we could eat out every night."

While that was certainly an option, one of the reasons we had rented an apartment in the first place was to have a choice between restaurants and a home-cooked meal. Since I liked to cook, I felt frustrated beyond belief and when it gradually hit me that the shopkeepers in Montparnasse hated Americans, I felt even worse. The only foreigners they seemed to hate more were the English and I was repeatedly asked if I were one or the other. This question was never accompanied by a smile or friendly expression, but by a sneer of naked contempt. When I said "American," I was rewarded with a look that implied it was the lesser of two evils but only by a slight margin. I longed to hurl back a snotty New York insult and spent hours at home looking up derogatory words in the Larousse, only to lose my nerve when the next opportunity presented itself.

Irritating as it was to wait on interminable lines, it was just as bad to be expected to spit out one's requirements with machine-gun speed when my turn came and yet that was the unspoken rule. As soon as the customer in front of me paid up, my stomach went into knots because I knew that only heaven could help me if I hesitated. A one-second delay and the people on line would begin to hiss and growl, while the shopkeeper's eyes turned to gray lead. I used to stay up late rehearsing what to say at the *poissonerie* the next day, that's how frantic and crazy I'd become.

Many of the French seemed to derive a morbid satisfaction from their own quick-fire requests for itsy-bitsy, teensy-weensy slivers of food that only a mouse could have made a meal of and although these requests were rampant, they reached the height of idiocy at the cheese shop. *Un morceau comme ça,* was a common refrain with the customer gleefully separating his thumb from his forefinger by the smallest fraction imaginable. This aroused in the shopkeeper an equally gleeful desire to cut the cheese at that precise measurement. If he failed by a hair, he apologized and sliced off more with the utmost deference. I waited for the day he sliced off his finger, but no such luck.

Since I refused to play this petty game, I defiantly began asking for huge amounts of everything. Six pounds of mushrooms, three dozen eggs, a tub of butter, all the Brie you have (motherfuckers). You would think that any shopkeeper would be happy to profit from my extravagance, but not on that street. After regaining their composure, their eyes filled with an even deeper contempt while the lynch mob behind me began to chant, "*Sal Americaine.*" On cheese days, I returned home a raving lunatic. "I hate the French!" I would cry. "Hate hate hate! Kill kill kill!"

"Don't you think you're overreacting a little?" John asked.

In a way he was right because even though the Montparnasse markets were ridiculous, my frustration had more to do with our sexual relationship than I wished to acknowledge. I had naïvely assumed that what started out as hesitant low-keyed lovemaking would gather momentum when we grew closer and more intimate in other areas. I was wrong. It didn't. In fact nothing about it changed, improved, or showed signs of doing so and the worst part was that John seemed happy with the status quo. At times, even smug. It finally occurred to me that he had no first-hand experience in the realm of heightened sensuality and therefore no way of knowing what we were missing.

I wanted to clear the air, but how? The subject was such a delicate one that I couldn't figure out the best way to broach it without hurting his pride. I was used to men who didn't need this kind of enlightenment, men whose very appearance telegraphed erotic expertise. Now that I thought about it, John telegraphed something quite different. Despite his good looks and abundance of charm, he came across as decidedly asexual. How had I missed it before? He treated women of all ages with the same show of chivalry and polite detachment that was guaranteed to keep them at arm's length, while his dealings with men were lusty and involved. It was with men that he argued, fought, philosophized, got drunk, wrestled in gutters, threw his arms around in greeting, slapped on the back, revealed his innermost thoughts to. It was with men that he was most himself. A horrible thought crossed my mind. What if John was gay? It was too much to bear. Drunk, cheap *and* gay?

I had been impatiently waiting for a reply from Sterling and at last it arrived. I shook when I opened the envelope, fearing the worst and the worst it was. Fawcett didn't like my revisions and was pulling out of the deal with Putnam. Without a softcover house to help defray costs, Sterling told me, Putnam was pulling out too. In short, *Getting Rid of Richard* was not going to be published, at least in the foreseeable future. "I feel like I've just been kicked in the stomach," I said to John.

"You have, but maybe Sterling will sell it to another publisher." He put his arms around me. "A better more enlightened publisher."

"I shouldn't have done those revisions without talking to the editors at Fawcett. I should have gone back to New York and sat down with them, found out what they really had in mind, tried to negotiate. I goofed."

I was also thinking that if I hadn't married John, if we hadn't moved to Paris, I would have been in New York when the Fawcett request for revisions came in, at which point I could have scooted over to their office and thrashed the whole thing out in person. Maybe the end result would have been the same, but now I would never know. "Be careful of what you want," the sages warned. I wanted to live in Paris. Was this the price I had to pay? Depression descended upon me, so thick and so black that it was an effort to get through the days. Seeking some sort of comfort, I began to eat and drink like a madwoman. Even though I loathed the local shopkeepers, I loved their food and the inexpensive *vin ordinaire* that was sold everywhere. Between the two I managed to pack more than twenty pounds onto my small-boned frame and went from slender to pudgy in a short amount of time.

"You've become a blimp in the fashion capital of the world," Walter Silver said to me one day. "I've never seen this side of you before. What gives, kiddo?"

"My sex life is at a standstill. My first novel has been rejected. My second novel is a disorganized mess. Everyone still asks if I paint, too, and my relations with the Montparnasse shopkeepers have hit an all time low. I find solace only at mealtimes."

"It doesn't sound good," Walter agreed. "But can't you try to cut back?"

"I don't want to cut back. I don't care how I look any more. I even had to let all my clothes out by hand." I showed him the expanded seams on my dress, the old stitch marks still visible. "John is too cheap to give me money for new clothes."

"What can I do to help?"

"Stick up a woman's clothing store. I'm a size fourteen these days."

Some mornings I didn't feel strong enough to face a barrage of shopkeepers' insults and that's when I began to patronize the small *laiterie* down the street from us. Even though the proprietor only sold milk, eggs and a limited variety of canned goods, it was better than nothing and easier on the nerves. People on the *laiterie* line seemed a little less hostile than those on the bustling avenue. After a few days, the heavyset woman behind the counter wanted to know if I was new to the quarter and what my husband did for a living. When I said he was a painter, she gave me the first smile I had ever received from a Parisian merchant. John couldn't believe it when I came home beaming.

I had been saving empty milk bottles for weeks as they were redeemable for a few francs apiece. One morning I stuffed ten of them into my faithful string bag and set out for the *laiterie*, feeling very thrifty and industrious. The line was extremely long that day. When my turn came, I placed the ten empties on the counter and asked for two bottles of milk. There was a collective gasp from the other customers while the woman behind the counter turned red with fury. "This is unheard of, Madame! Unbelievable! Unforgivable! Outrageous!"

I couldn't imagine what I had done wrong. Why did everyone look like they wanted to kill me? "Don't you have two bottles of milk?" I said.

"But of course," she replied, drawing herself up to her full imposing height. "That is not the issue, Madame, not the issue at all."

I wondered what the issue was. I was afraid to ask.

"You have the audacity to bring me ten empty bottles and then you ask me to only sell you *two* bottles?" She was spluttering by now. "Never in all my life have I heard such audacity. When one has ten empties, one buys ten bottles. Everyone knows that."

Now that the mystery was solved, I felt torn between laughter and suicide. Probably in the old days before milk was bottled, customers arrived carrying their own empty containers of varying sizes and whatever amount of liquid those containers held, that was the amount poured in and paid for. Out of that practical transaction, this insane one had evolved. Something inside me finally snapped. "You can sell me two bottles of milk, or you can sell me no bottles," I said, looking her squarely in the eye. "But if you think I'm taking these ten empties home, think again. I will smash them to bits right here on your floor before I do that. Do you understand?"

No one in the shop spoke, no one moved, no one seemed to breathe. My ultimatum had reduced the people in the *laiterie* to shocked immobility. It took the proprietor several seconds to reach a decision. "I will sell you two bottles of milk," she gravely replied.

"But I will do it only this time, Madame, and only because your husband is a painter." While walking back home, I thought of the difference in values between France and America. Being an artist here was considered prestigious, commendable. Being an artist in my country was considered suspect, shady. No wonder creative people gravitated to this side of the Atlantic where they were treated with respect and admiration, even if their wives were treated like dirt.

Just then I noticed the woman coming in my direction. It was Simone de Beauvoir probably going to her teaching stint at the Sorbonne. She seemed very brisk and professional, a briefcase in one hand, a reflective expression on her face (which was totally devoid of makeup). As we drew closer, she gave me a quick once-over and then glanced away. Did I imagine it or had I seen a glimmer of disdain in those sharp eyes? "I'm not what I appear to be," I wanted to say. "Despite this stupid string bag and two bottles of milk, I'm not your typical downtrodden housewife. I'm a novelist. My husband is a painter. All of our friends are involved in the arts. Basically I'm a very liberated woman."

And yet if that were true, I mused as she passed by, why was I financially dependent on John? Why was I the one who did all the marketing? Why didn't he ever help out? I mentioned this to him at dinner that same evening.

"I don't have time to buy groceries," he said. "I'm too busy painting."

"I suppose I could say that I'm too busy writing, but then we and the cats would starve. Do you think it's fair for me to get stuck with all the drudgery?"

"When you start supporting the household, I'll start going to the market." Maybe he was right. Maybe I would never be liberated until I was financially self-sufficient and could pay my own way. That's what he was saying. Mme. de Beauvoir had sized me up more accurately than I cared to admit.

My victory at the *laiterie* was short-lived because the very next day hostilities at the marketplace resumed all over again. When I tried to buy half a kilo of grapes, the man at the produce stall inexplicably refused to sell them to me. As he waved me off with an irritated gesture, I wondered how much more of this insolence I could take without exploding. That evening when John and I went out to dinner, painter Sam Francis stopped by our table to say hello. Sam had not only lived in Paris for years, he was shrewd. I described my problem and asked for his help.

"Say something in French," Sam told me. "Anything that comes to mind." After I had uttered a simple declarative sentence, he said, "Your accent is good, Joyce, but it's not perfect. Meaning it's not a bona fide Parisian accent, which is the only kind acceptable to these morons. So long as you continue trying to sound like them, they'll continue to demean and denigrate you."

"What should I do?"

"Stop speaking with a decent accent altogether. When you go to the market tomorrow, I want you to affect the flattest, dumbest American tones you can dredge up. Talk slowly, but clearly. Pretend you're from Iowa and learned French from a pocket Berlitz."

"What will that do?"

"It will tell the bastards that you're proud to be an American and you're not intimidated by their bullshit. Believe me, they'll never give you a hard time again. They're such sadomasochists, they'll be groveling at your feet for having outwitted them—just as they groveled at the Nazi's feet."

I flung my arms around him. "Sam, you're a genius."

The next day I decided to put it to the test at the *laiterie* before I tackled the major shops. When my turn came, I forced myself to speak the way Sam had instructed. "*Bonjour, Madame, deux litres du lait, s'il vous plait.*" I sounded like an American nitwit and it was all I could do to keep a straight face, but when I saw the proprietor's mouth fall open and her eyes narrow with suspicion I knew I had hit pay dirt.

"*Merci, Madame,*" she said in a more subdued voice than usual as she handed me the two bottles of milk.

I had won the first round and couldn't wait to go to the market later that afternoon. I needed to buy two chickens for a dinner party we were having. The man who killed the chickens gave me an insinuating once-over and asked if I was American or English. "American," I said, sharply.

"I guess that's a little better," he replied with the usual smirk.

My moment had come. "Do you know the mistake the Americans made during the war? We never should have liberated Paris. We should have let the Nazis blow you to smithereens. What do you think of that, you French imbecile?"

"You have no right to talk to me that way," he said, stunned by my outburst.

"*Au contraire*, I have every right. I'm sick of being humiliated by you and all the other shopkeepers on this street. I pay good money and what do I get in return? Nasty insults and sneering looks. Well, let me tell you something. You're not good enough to kiss an American's feet. Now pluck those chickens and keep your mouth shut."

Going to the market was a breeze after that.

Just as life was starting to look up, Martha Jackson arrived in Paris and wasted no time in marching over to our apartment with a surprising request. Maybe "command" would be a more appropriate word.

"I'm off to Spain for a couple of weeks and I want both of you to come with me. We'll fly to Barcelona, then hire and car and drive to Madrid with a few stops along the way. There are some painters whose work I'm anxious to see. I know that Joyce speaks Spanish, so that will be a big help."

John stared at the floor. I could feel his irritation and wondered why he didn't voice it. As for Martha, I doubt that it ever occurred to her we might not feel like going to Spain.

"We leave a week from today," she said, flashing a too-bright smile. "I'll call you with the details. I'm staying at the Ritz."

After she left, I confronted John. "You didn't say boo. Do you really want to make this trip?"

"There's no arguing with Martha."

"What does that mean?" I knew he hated to fly.

"It means we're going." He looked depressed. "Flying, if need be."

"Why does it mean that? What obligation do you have to this woman that compels you to jump at her every whim? I don't get it."

"She's my dealer. She's responsible for my success. I owe her something."

"From what you've told me about your history, Martha owes you something too." John had helped her start the gallery, had given her advice and encouragement back when she needed it the most. "Presumably you're even."

"She'll pay for the entire trip. It's not as though it's coming out of our pocket." To him, that seemed to justify it. "So what the hell?"

I thought of our expensive cabin on the *Liberté* and although John never admitted it, I knew that Martha had picked up the tab. Why? She wasn't by nature a generous person. In fact from what I had seen of her deals with others, she was a mean and stingy person. Did she use her money to keep John on a string? It was possible since his financial anxieties were enormous. While big mommy sure knew how to take advantage of a situation, she couldn't have succeeded without the cooperation of a certain insecure little boy.

"Why don't we pay our own way in Spain?" I asked.

"We can't afford to travel the way Martha does. She only goes first-class and I don't have that kind of money."

"Then maybe we shouldn't go."

We went. In addition to letting John talk me into it, I have to admit that Spain was the one country in Europe I most wanted to see. I also deluded myself that the trip might give me a chance to get to know Martha better, understand her quixotic behavior, hopefully come to some kind of understanding with this woman who was so important to my husband. I made arrangements with Walter and Libby to take care of the cats and started packing our suitcases, which still bore Italian train stickers. Enthusiasm was catching up with me, but not with John who became more and more depressed as the days flew by. "Why are you in such a bad mood?" I asked him. "You're the one who wanted to go."

"I never said I *wanted* to. I said I was going."

Once we set out, his depression worsened. Being under Martha's thumb almost every waking hour soon reduced him to zombie status. He showed no interest in anything, spoke only when absolutely necessary, never complained, never asserted himself, passively went along with whatever suggestions Martha made. I might not have existed for all the attention he paid to me. When I objected to Martha having booked adjoining suites at the Hotel Colón in Barcelona, he said, "What difference does it make?"

"Maybe we'd like some privacy. Don't you think that would occur to her Highness?"

"She probably doesn't want to be alone. Martha isn't as self-sufficient as she appears."

"I doubt if self-sufficiency has anything to do with it. She's paid for us and intends to get her money's worth."

"So? She's a businesswoman. What did you expect?" he replied to my astonishment.

For the five days that we were in Barcelona, John never tried to make love to me and I suspected he wouldn't until we got back to Paris. Big mommy might overhear us. While I could have taken the initiative, the truth was that Martha's imminent presence inhibited me too. We may as well have been children guiltily sharing *una cama matrimonial*, yet afraid to take advantage of it for fear of being caught in the act. Otherwise Barcelona was a joy. It was on the water, had a lot of energy, great seafood, as well as the whimsical Pare Guell designed by the city's beloved and idiosyncratic architect Antonio Gaudi.

One of Martha's painters, Antonio Tapies, was a native of Barcelona and spent hours showing us the sights. Despite the inane questions Martha asked him (in that grating voice) he was unfailingly polite. I could have sworn that I heard John gritting his teeth on more than occasion when Martha was being particularly obtuse, but he never spoke up. As for me, the highlight of the trip was the Catalan Museum with its extraordinary collection of paintings and sculpture.

Tapies was Catalan and told us that at home he and his wife spoke the regional dialect, not Spanish. Although Generalissimo Francisco Franco was at the height of his power then, we never mentioned his name or asked about his policies as it was common knowledge that Barcelona had always been a hotbed of anti-Franco sentiment, one word of which could get you arrested and thrown into prison without a trial. Fascist regimes like Franco's were ruthless and brutal. They didn't just kill dissenters, they tortured them first. Rumor had it that a favorite practice was cutting off prisoners' hands without benefit of an anesthetic. Once when I saw Tapies huddling with a lawyer and newspaper editor, I wanted to believe they were part of an underground resistance movement aimed at toppling the dreaded dictator.

We left for Madrid on a bright sunny morning with a hired car and driver. Enrique was in his fifties, well-mannered, dignified, nicely dressed in a gray suit and dark tie. Martha chose to sit up front next to him and for the next few hours never stopped bombarding him with questions regarding local points of interest, all of which Enrique (who spoke excellent English) informatively answered while John sulked in the back seat and I looked out the window. At last we reached the restaurant where Enrique had suggested we stop for lunch. After being shown to a table in the garden, Enrique held out Martha's chair but before he could sit down she waved him off. "Thank you, Enrique. That will be all."

Her dismissal was so rude and unwarranted that I felt myself flush with anger. I kicked John under the table expecting him to break his monolithic silence and give Martha a piece of his mind. Instead he looked away and kept quiet. I couldn't believe it. What was wrong with him? What kind of man had I married? I ordered a dry sherry and took it to the bar where Enrique was sipping an aperitif.

"Do you mind if I join you?"

"Please," he said. "Have a seat."

We drank our drinks and made small talk about the weather. He asked if I would like another sherry. I thanked him, but refused saying I had to return to my table. "I apologize for what she did," I told Enrique. "It was inexcusable."

He shrugged as though it wasn't the first time he had been shabbily treated by a tourist. "It's kind of you to say so, Señora."

Neither John nor Martha questioned me about what happened at the bar and we went on with our meal, but later when John and I were alone my resentment spilled out. "How could you just sit there and let her get away with it?" I asked him. "Don't you realize she publicly humiliated a decent intelligent man for no good reason? Enrique has more style in his little finger than Martha Jackson will ever see in her lifetime. Why didn't you tell her to knock it off?"

"It wouldn't have done any good. Martha can't eat with servants, it upsets her gallbladder condition."

"Enrique isn't a servant, he's a travel guide. And I noticed it didn't upset her gallbladder condition to sit next to him all day in the car and pick his brain about every cathedral and ruin we passed. Why do you keep defending that rude bitch?"

"It's not a matter of defending her, it's a matter of making the best of the situation. Martha is set in her ways."

"Well, I find her behavior outrageous."

"Then why don't you confront her?"

"Fine, I will." The only reason I had hesitated up until then was because I knew that a reprimand from John would carry more weight. The next morning when I told Martha that she was treating Enrique abominably by not letting him share our table at mealtime, she gave me a supercilious smile.

"If you had grown up with servants, Joyce, you would know that you're not expected to eat with them."

I looked at John, waiting for him to say that Enrique wasn't a servant. Now that I had gone on record, I hoped he would open his mouth and side with me. I thought wrong. He just sat there, staring off into space. We never discussed the matter again and for the rest of the trip Martha continued to dismiss Enrique at mealtimes, even if only a few minutes before they had been engaged in a spirited conversation. As a result of John's ongoing silence, I began to lose respect for him and by the time we reached Madrid we were barely on speaking terms. The fact that the city was experiencing a ninety-degree heatwave didn't improve our dispositions.

"Let's find a shoe store," I said on our second day there. "I have to buy a pair of sandals."

"Why do you need sandals all of a sudden?"

"Why do you think? To make walking bearable in this oven of a city." We were coming out of the Palace Hotel where Martha had reserved adjoining suites for a change. "All I have are these pumps and my feet are killing me."

"Spend, spend, spend! That's all you know. Here, take all my money!" To the surprise of passing pedestrians, John emptied his pockets and pesetas tumbled out onto the sidewalk. "Go ahead, pick them up. What are you waiting for?"

"You're an anal-retentive cheapskate. You've got hemorrhoids because you're too cheap to part with a buck. Freud would have had a field day with you."

"You want bucks? Here are some bucks." He removed a wad of bills from his wallet and threw them on the ground. "Go buy your sandals. Clean me out. Bleed me dry. What do I care? Spend, spend, spend!"

I bought the least expensive sandals I could find and regretted ever having come on this trip. In addition to our personal problems, I was uncomfortable in Madrid. As the seat of government, the presence of Franco and his dictator's regime could be felt more keenly than in any other city we had visited. The Guardia Civil arrogantly strutted around in their fascist uniforms and distinctive three-cornered hats, secure in a carte blanche power to intimidate the most law-abiding citizen by throwing him into one of the dreaded prisons without formal charges, trial, or legal representation. Even the famed Prado paled after the glories of the Catalan Museum and it was a relief to head north.

Martha had booked rooms in the picturesque resort town of Cadaques on the Costa Brava, saying she wanted to go see Salvador Dali who had a house nearby. She asked us to accompany her. Unfortunately Dali wasn't home the day we dropped by, so I missed my chance to meet the world's most famous living surrealist. It was in Cadaques that Martha verbalized her true feelings about me. We were alone on the beach one morning when she suddenly said, "You should be grateful that someone as talented, handsome and wonderful as John married you. I mean who are you, Joyce? You can't even get a book published. You're a nobody."

I wanted to pick her up and drown her in the Mediterranean. (Ironically, she drowned in a swimming pool in Los Angeles years later, because of a heart attack.) "Who am *I*?" I said. After the Montparnasse markets, I was through being intimidated. "That's a hot one. The real question, Martha, is who are *you*? A rich bitch idiot who has the art world tyrannized with her sadistic ploys, but since I'm not part of that world I don't have to be nice to you. I don't want anything from you. In fact I despise you and if you ever talk to me like that again, I will kill you. Got it?"

"You certainly have a temper," she said with a blinding smile.

Later John asked what I had done to upset Martha. "Nothing much," I replied. "I just threatened to kill her if she gave me any more grief."

"You take her too seriously. Ignore the woman. Half the time she doesn't know what she's talking about."

"*You* ignore her. That's your specialty. I've had it with Miss Looneytunes. After we get back to Paris, I never want to lay eyes on her again."

I didn't have to. Martha returned to New York immediately, leaving John and me alone with our problems. I knew they weren't going to be resolved when he started drinking heavily as soon as we settled in. At first it was just beer and wine, but before long he had switched to hard liquor for which his capacity was astonishingly low. A few drinks and he was blotto. He once had had hepatitis and his liver could no longer metabolize alcohol, yet that didn't stop him from throwing back Negronis (a lethal combination of gin, dry vermouth and Compari) until he passed out cold.

The next thing I knew it was August when anyone with any money abandoned the city to the hordes of descending tourists. Walter and Libby were going to tour Scotland by car and asked us to join them, but John and I couldn't face the ordeal of being thrown into each other's company twenty-four hours a day with no possibility of escape, so we declined. With the rest of our friends also gone, John became chummy with a Dutch painter named Teeck who could drink sailors under tables. Pretty soon the two of them were going on three-day benders from which Teeck seemed to emerge relatively unscathed, but not my husband who came home a physical wreck.

All of my pleas that he stop drinking fell on deaf ears and I realized it was only a matter of time before his body gave way. It happened near the end of August. Teeck dragged John home one sunny afternoon, holding him up to keep him from collapsing. "You'd better put him to bed," the Dutchman said before he left. "He's had it, the poor bastard."

Slumped in a chair at the end of the long trestle table, John was ashen and wild eyed. "If you ever get out of this alive, Hillary, go back to San Francisco."

I had never been to San Francisco but his first wife, Hillary, had been born there. John met her there and they lived in Sausalito when they were married. He was hallucinating. As he babbled on about my going back to San Francisco, I wished that Walter and Libby were around for advice. Even Hemi Fara was gone, having taken off for a holiday in Portugal. Finally I picked up the phone and called the only person who could bail us out of this mess. I told Martha that John was in terrible shape and would only get worse if we remained in Paris.

"How terrible is terrible?" she asked.

"I've never seen him like this." In the background, I could hear her parrot screaming, "ABSTRACT EXPRESSIONISM IS HERE TO STAY." "We need money to return to New York. At least there he has you and his psychiatrist."

"Are you sure that returning is the best course of action?"

"He's been drunk for days, Martha. No. Weeks. If we don't leave soon, he'll wind up in a straightjacket. He thinks I'm Hillary."

That did it. "I'll wire the money right away."

Maneuvering John up the stairs and into bed was no mean feat and I wished I had thought to ask Teeck to do it. I tried to get him to lean on me, but his balance was so unsteady and he was so much heavier than I that I was afraid he would fall down the stairs and break a leg. Finally by going very slowly, we made it and once under the covers he remained there. I brought his meals up on a tray, let him sleep around the clock, and slowly the color began to return to his cheeks. When I felt he was strong enough to deal with it, I told him about my phone call to Martha.

"You made the right decision," he said. "We have to go home."

"I was afraid you'd be angry with me since we came to stay and even signed a lease on this apartment."

"I'm not angry, I'm relieved. The lease doesn't matter." He gave me a weak smile. "Do you think I could get a glass of milk?"

"Sure, just as soon as I buy some. We're all out."

I walked down the street to the *laiterie* and wearily got on line, an old timer by now. In the windowpane I caught of glimpse of myself: fat, badly-dressed, the seams on my skirt about to burst, my hair in need of a trim, my shoes run down at the hells, yet for once I didn't give a damn. I thought of how anxious I had been about this city, its intimidating chic, its hostile shopkeepers, Simone de Beauvoir's opinion of me, my clothes, my hairdo, my weight, my inability to speak the language properly. "*Bonjour, Madame,*" I said to the proprietor in my fractured French. "*Deux litres du lait, s'il vous plait.*"

Why do we always worry about the wrong things, I wondered?

Campello: 1973

I NEVER intended to go to Spain in the first place. I intended to move to London, lock, stock, and barrel. I was fed up with New York. The crime rate had gotten so out of hand that women's purses were being snatched on Madison Avenue in broad daylight, in addition to which I didn't want to remain in a country where Richard Nixon was president. Besides, I could afford to move abroad, my financial situation having improved drastically since when I lived in Paris when Sterling Lord couldn't sell my first novel and as a result, I was financially dependent on my second husband, painter John Hultberg.

What a difference fourteen years had made! Since then I'd had five books published, one of them (*The Crazy Ladies*) a runaway bestseller from which I was still receiving royalties. While it took much longer than I ever anticipated to see my writing efforts pay off, it finally happened so that at the age of forty-three I was my own woman, beholden to no one. It was a heady feeling, even though I was beginning to discover some of the downsides to independence. For one thing I no longer seemed to attract successful men, but men who were either broke or lacking ambition and were dazzled by my success. I had never been in that position before and after a while I became suspicious of the motives of every man who showed an interest. Was he attracted to me or to the fact that I had money? It made me realize how a wealthy man might react when a woman came onto him. Did she really like him for himself or was she a gold digger?

The same questions now crossed my mind and were unsettling. I wasn't used to thinking of men in those terms. Corny as it may sound today, I was used to thinking of them in terms of guidance and protection but suddenly no man felt I needed his guidance or protection since I had the aura of money to protect me. That I was still the same emotionally needy woman I had always been never seemed to occur to any of them, the glow of success distorting my image. And when I did meet somebody who was well-heeled, I detected an undercurrent of resentment. At first I wondered if I was imagining it, Then one day the businessman I had been dating confirmed my suspicions.

"I admire you, Joyce, but there's nothing I can give you that you can't buy for yourself," he said after we had been seeing each other for several months. "It makes me uncomfortable, so I think we should call it quits."

I hadn't expected this and was dismayed. "When you say there's nothing you can give me, you're thinking in materialistic terms. What about love and affection? I can't buy those."

"True, but I find it hard to love a woman who doesn't need me in the usual ways."

"What ways are those?"

"Call me a male chauvinist pig, but I've always been the breadwinner in the family and with you, I'm not. For all I know, you make more money than I do."

He was in the import-export business and had a habit of running around the Caribbean with hundreds of thousands of dollars in an attaché case. "Even if that's true, which I doubt, so what?"

"So I can't handle it. I'm sorry."

Had we met years ago when I was still trying to get a book published, he probably would have fallen in love with the poor struggling writer I was back then. He would have wanted to help me, advise me, take care of me, be the big strong generous man in my life, a man I could lean on. That I would still like to lean on him occasionally never crossed his mind, which made me sad. Did I really appear that self-sufficient? I found it hard to believe because *I* hadn't changed. Only my circumstances had. So with this last romance on the rocks and my sixth book (*The Three of Us*) recently completed, there was nothing to keep me in New York. Besides, I had spent some time in London a few years before and felt I could be happy living there. From what I had seen of the English, I admired their lifestyle which was less frenzied than ours and also placed less emphasis on the glories of youth. I never felt like a grownup in my own country, only in older civilizations where adults were treated with respect. The time had come to pull up roots.

Then my plans unexpectedly changed due to my friend, Joan Zetka, who was tired of waiting for her long lost love (Bela von Block) to leave his wife in Venice and come live with her. Joan hadn't heard from Bela in months and felt as strongly as I did about the crime rate on the home front, so when an acquaintance at the Spanish Consulate offered to rent her his condo on the Mediterranean for five hundred dollars a year, she took him up on it sight unseen. Later she told me she was dying to have a year off to devote to her painting, which had been put on hold because of her nine-to-five job at Asia House.

"Why don't I go to Spain with you and help you get settled?" I said, impulsively. I knew that Joan had never lived abroad and didn't speak Spanish.

"Then I'll take off for London as originally planned."

The idea seemed to please her.

"Let's go by ship," I suggested. "Not only can you bring tons of stuff, but a leisurely ocean voyage will be fun. We'll sit on deck chairs covered by lap robes and wait for the steward to come around with hot bouillon. We'll travel first-class and dress for dinner. We'll dance to a live band."

"I can't afford first-class. I have to watch every penny."

"Let's see how much it will cost before you say no."

In the end Joan succumbed and we booked passage months in advance on the *Raffaelo*, the only ocean liner in operation at the time with a sailing date set for the second week in April 1973. Then one evening while the two of us were having dinner with an ex-boyfriend of Joan's, her phone rang. "Hello," Bela von Block said. "I'm in

New York. I've left Sylvia. I'm coming over."

Joan's mouth fell open. It was the last thing she had expected, but before she could say a word Bela hung up. An hour later in he walked carrying a huge bouquet of flowers and wearing an anticipatory smile, which soon disappeared when she told him she was going to Spain for a year. The ex-boyfriend and I sat there watching Bela try to come to terms with what he obviously considered a ridiculous decision. "Spain?" he said with a derisive laugh. "What are you talking about? I just got here. You can't go to Spain."

"Sorry, but I am," Joan said.

"No, you damn well are not."

"Watch me."

The ex-boyfriend and I left quietly when Bela called her "a crazy broad" and then spent the next few months trying to change her mind, but Joan had already given notice at Asia House and arranged for a friend to take care of her toy poodle. She had also paid Juan Cassals, her Spanish Consulate acquaintance, five hundred dollars for the year's rent.

"None of that matters," Bela declared. "You don't need a job because you'll be living with me and as for the five hundred bucks, big deal. Now call the Italian Line and cancel the reservation."

When she refused, he alternated between begging her to come to her senses and hurling malevolent curses at her, all the while declaring his undying love. "I've left my wife for you," he would cry. "Doesn't that prove how serious and committed I am?"

"Why didn't you tell me in advance that you were going to leave Sylvia," Joan asked. "You never said a word. In fact I hadn't heard a peep out of you in months, then suddenly you show up and say, 'Hello, I'm here.' And you wonder why I'm reluctant to change my plans?"

"Okay, I admit I may have gone about this the wrong way but is that any reason to desert me now that I've decided I love you and can't live without you?"

"I love you, too, but I'm going to Spain with Joyce."

"Screw Joyce," said my friend Bela who had me to thank for meeting Joan in the first place. "She can go by herself."

"No, she can't. The condo is in my name and, besides, she's only coming along to help me get settled. Then she's moving to London."

"Why didn't you say so before? That simplifies everything. Joyce can go straight to London and you can stay here with me."

"My mind is made up, Bela. I'm going to Spain."

"Grrrrrrrrr."

Around this time I was taking tennis lessons, which in retrospect seems pretty ridiculous because I was drinking too much to hit the ball most days. Having tried (and failed) to kick booze, maybe I thought that learning how to play tennis would prove I was in better shape than I appeared. I don't know. My addiction to alcohol had crept up slowly and still surprised me because for so many years I was a mild social drinker. In fact when I was married to both my alcoholic husbands, if anyone had said I would eventually follow in their footsteps I would have laughed.

And yet as soon as I got a contract to write *The Crazy Ladies* and quit my office job, my drinking began to escalate. It was almost as though it had been in abeyance for years because I had to remain sober during the day in order to type all the correspondence my employer required. And don't forget I'm referring to a time when there were no computers, only electric typewriters which entailed very careful typing (often with three carbon copies) or else it meant tearing up the page and starting over. One drink at lunchtime would have destroyed my coordination and I wasn't about to risk it, but once I could stay home all day and write any old time I pleased, my drinking went haywire.

One Wednesday in mid-February I felt even more hungover than usual and decided to cancel my weekly tennis lesson. "I can't make it today," I told my coach over the phone. Then I faltered and added, "Someone very close to me has just died."

After we hung up, I began to shake. I hadn't planned to lie about someone dying and couldn't account for the sense of dread that gripped me. A little while later when I went downstairs to get the mail, there was a letter from an old friend, Danny Banko, who had moved to Florida. In his opening sentence, he said that my first husband had died of cirrhosis of the liver. John was forty-eight and had been drinking heavily since his teens. Having run into him several years ago, I realized that he had lost not only his good looks but his mind as well. He babbled on and on, talking gibberish, making no sense. At first I couldn't understand it, but later learned it was known as having "a wet brain," the end result of a lifetime of alcoholic excess.

John's death had a devastating effect on me inasmuch as he was the first man I ever loved (according to some friends, the *only* man) and I couldn't believe he was gone. Danny Banko claimed that John's doctor had warned him if he didn't go on the wagon, he would be dead in no time. "So what?" was John's alleged reply. An iconoclast to the bitter end. Did this incident scare me into sobriety? Don't be silly. Cirrhosis of the liver would never get me, I rationalized. I took tons of Vitamin B.

As the time approached for our departure, Joan was turning into a nervous wreck not only because of Bela's non-stop harassment but because of her own increasing ambivalence. That she stuck to her guns in spite of everything drove Bela nuts. I knew he was used to getting his own way and accepted defeat badly, which in my experience most men did since they're brought up to win whereas women are brought up to compromise. I half-expected Joan to cave in at the last minute, yet she stood firm and as the date of embarkation grew nearer we became so excited that we decided to throw a bon voyage party the Saturday morning of our sailing.

Although we sent out loads of invitations, we didn't expect most people to show up due to the early hour. Not only did they show up, they brought others along: spouses, children, friends, lovers, house guests. The Michaelangelo Room at the pier was jammed with smiling well wishers guzzling Asti Spumante, many of them saying they wanted to run away too and admired our adventurous spirit. The only non-smiling person was Bela, who wore an angry scowl while Joan's eyes were red from crying. She told me that she had spent a terrible night with Bela still attempting to persuade her to change her mind and when he didn't succeed, he raved and ranted for hours afterward. She had barely slept a wink.

"You'll sleep on the ship," I said. "He won't be able to harass you there."

Which showed how little I knew both about ships and Bela von Block.

For the next five days and four nights, Bela never stopped calling Joan and she seemed to spend more time in the Radio Room, which was located on the top deck and accessible only by elevator, than she did in our cabin or the dining room. We were sharing a table with four other passengers and no sooner did we sit down to breakfast, lunch or dinner than an announcement would come over the loudspeaker requesting Ms. Zetka to go to the Radio Room for a ship-to-shore telephone call. Upon her return, Joan's face would have dropped five inches and it was apparent she had been crying. The second night out one of the other passengers, an elderly woman, turned to me in concern. "What's wrong with your friend?" she asked. "She looks so upset every time she comes back. Is someone back home sick?"

"Only romantically. Her fiancé is giving her a hard time for leaving New York."

"Where are you girls headed?"

Girls? Joan and I were in our early forties. "Spain. The Costa Blanca. A small village called Campello. Joan will be fine once we get there. There's no telephone in our condo."

Joan told me that Bela had been drinking when he called and spent the entire time hurling insults at her for deserting him. When I asked what he expected her to do about it in mid-ocean, she said she didn't know but that he was more furious than ever, miserable, bereft.

"In that case, why don't you ask him to get on the next plane and meet us in Spain?"

"He would love to, but he's doing revisions on *Oil* and apparently there's no end in sight. Every time he sends in one batch of new pages, his editor asks for more. Bela says it's an ongoing nightmare."

I was surprised he didn't put his foot down. "The next time you talk to him, tell him not to capitulate on every one of his editor's requests. As the writer Bela has the last word and since he's a pro, I'm sure he knows that."

"I don't think he does," Joan said.

Oil was probably Bela von Block's eightieth book, most of which he wrote under a pseudonym as he was doing with this one. Jonathan Black was his latest moniker, although at various times in his colorful career he had been Dr. W. D. Sprague, Ph.D., Leo Vernon, Aldo Lucchesi, Ilya Chambertin (for a series of astrology books even though Bela didn't believe in astrology), and my favorite name of all, Carolyn Hennessey, author of *I, B-I-T-C-H*. In addition he had ghostwritten all of the J. Paul Getty books and *Playboy* articles bearing Mr. Getty's name. When I first met Bela, he told me that if necessary he could grind out a book in three weeks. I was impressed. "How can you write that fast?" I asked him.

"I take benzedrine and stay up all night. It's no big deal."

"Maybe not to you. I could take benzedrine until it came out of my ears and I couldn't finish a book in three weeks."

"That's because you've never tried. Besides, they're not very long books, only about two hundred and fifty pages in manuscript."

"Are you kidding? That's approximately twelve pages a day. The most I've ever done in my life was seven pages and I considered that pretty good."

"You're more serious about writing than I am. These quickie books I write aren't exactly great literature."

"Neither are mine and they take a lot longer."

"My mistake was leaving the Army," Bela mused. "Had I stayed in, I'd be retired by now with a sizable pension and wouldn't have to worry about getting an idea for my next book. I would be financially set for life."

"Don't you enjoy the writing process at all?"

"No, I hate it. What's there to enjoy? It's torture."

"I was thinking about all the discoveries."

"What discoveries?"

"I learn things when I write—about myself, about life, about other people. It's a fascinating journey of revelation."

"You're a real writer," said the man who had published over eighty books. "I'm just a hack."

My drinking aboard the *Rafaello* had been very moderate but after Joan and I disembarked at Algeciras and checked into the Reina Cristina Hotel with its breathtaking view of the Rock of Gibraltar, I suddenly began drinking like a lunatic all over again. Why? I don't know any more than I knew why I didn't drink that way when were out at sea, unless there was something about the regimented schedule that kept my intake to a minimum. All I know for sure is that with an alcoholic, there is no logical time to start drinking. Anytime is the logical time. Any excuse will do. Any place is the right place. Any drink is the right drink. And without warning, all bets are off. Joan was upset by this abrupt reversal and began giving me dirty looks whenever I asked room service to bring me another rum and coke. The waiter was delighted as I tipped him lavishly every time he came waltzing up to our room.

"Let's go to Tangier," I urged Joan after I had downed five of the potent rum concoctions. "It's a short ferry ride and we'll never have this chance again."

Before she could reply, the phone rang. We exchanged startled glances, wondering who it could be since we hadn't known in advance where we were staying. Surprise! It was Bela. He had tracked us down, having deduced that the Reina Cristina was the only good hotel in Algeciras, whereupon there ensued another heated exchange with him ranting and raving from New York. Joan just shook her head as tears filled her eyes. Sober I might have been sympathetic, but half-bombed I found Bela's obsession with her highly amusing and couldn't help laughing.

"You think this is funny?" Joan snapped afterward.

"Hilarious. Face it, kiddo, there's no escape from him. He would find you even if you tried to disappear into darkest Africa. He's crazy about you. Now can we go to Tangier?"

"I'm not going anywhere with you. I'm too depressed and you're too drunk."

"Oh come on, Joan. Think of it. Tangier. Maria Montez. The souks. The medina. Arab decadence. You'll never forgive yourself if you pass up this opportunity."

"Let me alone," she said, brushing away a tear.

"How are we going to get to Campello?" she asked the next day. "We have so much stuff that I'm beginning to think it wouldn't even be feasible to go by train."

"Probably not. Let's hire a car."

"It's a long trip." She had been looking at maps of the area. "Won't it cost a fortune?"

"Nothing in Spain costs a fortune. This is one of the cheapest countries in Europe and also one of the safest, for which we can thank a fascist dictatorship. I'll bet if we hire a car for ourselves and a small truck for our luggage, it will cost less than a good restaurant meal in New York."

"Even with everything I have?"

"That's my guess."

Joan's luggage was indeed formidable consisting of two footlockers, two bulky steamer trunks and three large suitcases into which she had crammed every piece of clothing she owned, as well as sheets, pillowcases, blankets and towels. Bela, who had lived abroad for years, told her to take them since they were much more expensive in Europe. By comparison I was traveling light with only a few suitcases since I had shipped most of my belongings to be put in storage in London. I didn't expect to stay in Spain long, a month tops, by which time I felt sure that Joan would be able to manage on her own providing she improved her Spanish. To date, her grasp of the language was limited to phrases like, "*El actor es popular.*"

"That will get you far," I said.

Arranging for transportation to Campello proved easy when it turned out that the man who had a car for hire had a cousin with a truck, whereupon we made plans to leave early the next morning. Our driver said the trip would take at least ten hours since we would be passing through mountainous terrain. Before we turned in that night, I asked Joan if she was nervous about the condo she had rented sight unseen and would be occupying for the next year.

"A little nervous," she admitted. "But Juan said it overlooks the Mediterranean, so how bad can it be?"

We left Algeciras at eight the next morning and didn't arrive in Campello until ten that night, the mountainous terrain being even more extensive and torturous than our driver had anticipated. Some of the roads were so full of twists and turns that it was hard not to fear imminent disaster, especially with other drivers zooming along at breakneck speed. Spaniards seemed to drive the way Mexicans did and I was reminded of my first trip south of the border nearly twenty years before when I was young and married to my first husband. Try as I did to mentally connect with the woman I was back then, she refused to come into focus. Maybe it was too painful to remember how hopeful she had been, all of her disillusionments still to come.

I also didn't want to remember how much I liked being with a man, feeling loved and protected, relieved that I didn't have to make all the decisions by myself or assume total responsibility for every aspect of my existence. I missed the way men responded to problems, which was different from the way women did. (Men tended to act, women to ponder.) I missed their directness, I missed that special masculine energy more than I cared to admit and wondered if I would ever have it again.

Our first glimpse of the five-hundred-dollar-a-year Mediterranean condo was not auspicious. For one thing, two of Juan Cassall's aunts greeted us at the door swathed in black and wearing expressions of reproach because of the late hour of our arrival. Their welcome was cold as they led us inside and then with a flourish of her hand, one aunt said, "Well, Señoras, here it is!"

Joan's mouth dropped open in horror and I could see why. A big dining table sat smack in the center of the living room and was covered with an ugly piece of oilcloth, while the rest of the terrible furniture was lined up against the walls. The only illumination came from a low-wattage naked light bulb that dangled overhead. Otherwise the small two-bedroom apartment was plunged in darkness and although we could hear waves lapping against the shore down below, we couldn't see the Mediterranean. When I asked the aunts if we might have something to eat after our long journey, they grudgingly offered us a bottle of warm beer. As I accepted it, I heard Joan whisper that she couldn't possibly live here, not in a million years, and now what was she going to do?

"Don't despair," I said after the aunts had retreated to the kitchen to guard their cache of food. "It will look different in the morning when the sun is shining and the two witches leave for Madrid. We'll move the table off to one side, buy some nice wicker chairs, rugs, plants, local pottery, a pretty cotton tablecloth. We'll fix the joint up. You'll never recognize it, Joan."

I thought she was going to cry, but she didn't. She just stood there with a miserable expression on her face. We had to share a bedroom that night since the aunts were in the other one, but by morning they were gone and sunlight flooded the apartment. Stepping out onto the small terrace, we had a clear view of the blue Mediterranean which was dazzling in its intensity.

"You were right," Joan said. "It's starting to look different already. Let's move that damn table."

Although it was heavier than it looked, as soon as we had shoved it back against the wall the room seemed to magically open up and suggest some interesting decorative possibilities. As a painter with a keen eye, Joan saw that even more clearly than I did and smiled for the first time since we arrived in Campello.

If everything was dirt cheap in Spain, alcohol was even cheaper. There was a bodega in town (a store that only sold liquids) where you could fill your own bottle at any one of a number of huge vats. Although Scotch and bourbon were relative costly, gin and rum went for a dollar a quart. I couldn't believe it. In addition the *portero* (concierge) who ran a small grocery store on the ground floor of our building, sold wine for twenty-five cents a bottle. So what if it was a little raw to the palate? When Joan saw me throwing it back like there was no tomorrow, she said that in Algeciras I had promised to quit drinking. Since I couldn't remember saying anything so foolish, I told her that considering the local prices I couldn't afford to quit. It was a remark she would remind me of for the rest of my life.

Our white eight-story building named "Cabo Azul" (Blue Cape) had been built on the Mediterranean shoreline in the early Sixties and is undoubtedly worth a fortune today, but like everything else in Spain at the time it was very inexpensive. Much of the beachside adjoining Cabo Azul was devoid of housing of any kind (reminding me of the afternoon beach in Acapulco in 1954) and after a late dinner out, Joan and I often walked home along the deserted road without fear of assault or robbery. To attack a woman in Spain in those days, especially if she were a tourist, was to risk being thrown into one of Franco's dreaded prisons for an indefinite stay. Torture and limb amputation were routine punishments that no man in his right mind was willing to chance, certainly not with the Guardia Civil patrolling the area. Once when I awakened around dawn and happened to glance out the window, I saw about ten of them engaged in target practice. Wearing their distinctive military uniform, they stood lined up in a row, soldiers proud, firing their weapons into the sea. The sound was deafening.

Within days of our arrival, telegrams from Bela began pouring in by the carload. Had there been a phone in our condo, I'm sure he would have been on it incessantly but since there was a long waiting list for such amenities in the primitive village of Campello, a post office messenger would park his motor scooter at Cabo Azul and take the elevator to our top-floor abode. "*Tengo una telegrama para Sra. Zetka,*" he would announce, his face wreathed with excitement as he handed Joan a neatly folded piece of blue paper. Apparently it was a rare event in those parts to receive even one telegram, let alone the influx that soon began bombarding Joan.

"Bela wants me to return to New York immediately," she told me after reading what was probably the fifth telegram. "He says he's going crazy without me and doesn't know how much longer he can continue to function if I stay in Spain."

At the end of every telegram, he begged her to call him in New York at such and such a time or he wouldn't be responsible for what happened next. In order to make this call, we had to go into Campello (either by foot or bus) and give the Hotel Royalton number to an old crone who worked in the hole-in-the-wall telephone office. Then Joan would sit in a small booth with a beaded curtain door and wait for the ancient black contraption to ring, while I paced around outside. When she emerged, she would shake her head as if to say it had been more of the same and not worth repeating. Since these calls invariably took place in the middle of the afternoon Spanish time, so as to reach Bela in the morning New York time, the shops in town were closed for siesta and we would shlep back to Cabo Azul.

Meanwhile my drinking had gotten so out of control that Joan finally said if she had known how addicted I was, she never would have agreed to letting me share the condo. I asked her how it was possible for her *not* to know considering that we lived next door to each other in New York and saw each other constantly. "There's a big difference between living next door and living on top of each other," she replied. "You drink all the time, Joyce, I've never seen anything like it. I'm just surprised that your right hand hasn't become deformed from clutching a glass."

"If it bothers you that much, don't look."

"Even if I didn't look, I could smell you three miles away."

"Pinch your nose."

"If that your quaint way of tell me you have no intention of cutting back?"

"I can't cut back," I said, pouring another drink. "I've tried." Drinking to me was as natural as breathing and more much satisfying. I didn't need to be upset about something in order to numb myself into oblivion (not that I couldn't find something to be upset about if I put my mind to it), nor did I need to be unhappy. I could be happy, unhappy, it could be sunny or cloudy, rainy or dry, winter or summer, good times or bad and I would reach for a drink. That's what alcoholics do. As I learned many years later, we don't drink because our problems are worse than anyone else's, we drink because we're alcoholics.

This is not to say that once in Spain I wasn't at loose ends, since I was, and yet had I stayed in New York I would also have been at loose ends and reaching for a drink, the only thing that kept me relatively sane having vanished. I refer to my routine of spending long hours at the typewriter, working on a new book. But because I had finished a book (*The Three of Us*) just before leaving for Spain, I was now in the dreaded post-partum period, a stretch of time that has always been difficult for writers (even those who aren't alcoholics) for two main reasons.

One, the main focus of your existence is gone, and two, you're afraid you will never get another creative idea and never write another book as long as you live. It doesn't matter how many books you've published or how successful you are, the fear of drying up is classic, universal. Having always been intrigued by what other writers did when faced with this situation, I discovered that they either traveled or, if they were lucky, started another book. I had tried traveling, but instead of it lifting my depression I found myself depressed in a foreign country without any of the creature comforts of home. As for starting another book so quickly, I could no more do it than I could fly to the moon unaided, so I envied those writers who were more resilient. I would have given anything to change places with them.

Now if I weren't an alcoholic, I might have decided to leave for London sooner than planned. Or I might have explored the attractive seaport city of Alicante, which was only a bus ride away. Or I might have taken up sailing, deep sea fishing, snorkeling, any number of sporting activities I could have afforded. Therefore it pains me to admit that the only thing I could think of doing was to drink. While it seems very unimaginative, I often feel that I put all of my imagination into my books and have none left over for my life.

By the end of May, Joan at last succumbed to Bela's repeated demands that she return to New York—or else!

"Or else what?" I asked her.

"Who knows? But I think I'd better go back."

"For how long?" Even though we were still at loggerheads over my drinking, the idea of being without someone to talk to or share a meal with was daunting.

"I don't know how long I'll stay," she said. "I'll see when I get there."

We went to dinner that evening at a restaurant called La Querencia (a bullfighting term) where I proceeded to get smashed and inadvertently left my purse at the bar. I didn't realize what I had done until the next morning when I was getting dressed as in my deranged hungover state, I had decided to accompany Joan to the Alicante airport and ride back to Campello with the cabdriver. Then it hit me that my missing purse contained not only all my cash and credit cards, but a foreigner's most valued possession: my passport. Joan looked stricken when I told her the news.

"Not to worry," I said. "If this were France or Italy, I could kiss that purse goodbye. But here in fascist Spain, I'll bet you anything that the manager of La Querencia drives up in a little while and personally returns it to me."

That's exactly what happened after I got back to Cabo Azul with the cabdriver who couldn't believe how drunk I was. In Spain, it was unheard of for a woman to be drunk, at least not in public and certainly not flaunting it. "*Borracha*," he kept saying, pointing at me and grinning. "*Borracha.*"

As it turned out, Joan was gone for six weeks during which time I had no idea what to do with myself. She and I were the only Americans for miles around and although there was an English colony living nearby, most of them struck me as dull and provincial, the dregs of England with whom I had nothing in common except a shared language. I decided I would rather tough it out alone than join them dancing the Scottish reel or eating bangers and mash as if they were still in Bournemouth. But after a few weeks as I was quietly going crazy, I met Juan Lozano. He was the local repairman, plumber, electrician, and jack of all trades. The *portero*'s beady-eyed husband hadn't been able to fix Joan's sink that became stopped up shortly after her departure, so it was Juan Lozano to the rescue.

Although fairly small in stature, Juan was nice-looking, polite, well-educated and, having been born in Casablanca where many Spaniards fled after the Republican cause lost the Civil War, he spoke French in addition to Spanish. While he didn't know a word of English, that was okay since my Spanish (if not my French) had improved by then. I could tell that Juan found me attractive and after fixing Joan's sink in no time flat, he invited me to dinner. Grateful for the company, I agreed. I have little recollection of our first date, I only remember that two nights later we were screwing our brains out after dancing to Joan's extensive collection of Frank Sinatra records. Juan was an accomplished and sensitive lover, but what I really liked about him were the sexual phrases he taught me that weren't to be found in any Spanish dictionary. Upon my insistence, he provided translations for: gay man, lesbian, I'm coming, I didn't come, would you go down on me, would you like me to go down on you? And my favorite—my, what a big penis you have.

The next thing I knew, Juan had fallen in love with me before he realized the full extent of my drinking and when he did, he was appalled. One evening in desperation he poured every bottle of booze I owned down the sink while I stood by and laughed. When he wanted to know what was so funny, I said, "Your thinking that that will stop me."

"You should stop, Joyce. You're killing yourself."

"I know, but why is it taking so long?"

He wasn't amused. As a Capricorn Juan Lozano regarded life as serious business, whereas to me it was a freak show. A few weeks into our romance, he said he wanted to marry me. "I will build a house high up on a mountain in a remote locale, so we can shut out the world and be alone. Just the two of us. How does it sound?"

Terrible, I felt like saying. "You're a true Capricorn, Juan, the goat climbing the proverbial mountain. Astrologers would love you."

"What does that mean?"

"I'm moving to London."

His face darkened. "When?"

"Soon."

"Why didn't you tell me this before?"

"It never came up."

He was furious. "You didn't think I deserved to know?"

"Not at first. I mean we weren't serious at first."

"*I* was serious."

What could I say? That I wasn't? I didn't want to hurt his feelings. He was a nice guy. He just wasn't the kind of guy I intended to spend the rest of my life with—or the rest of the year, for that matter. How was I going to get out of this one gracefully, I wondered? Joan Zetka, where are you? Unfortunately still in New York arguing with Bela. Since I didn't see Juan until the evening, I had long days with nothing to except go to the beach, go to town, and go to Ted & Terry's Bar which was on the way to town.

Ted and Terry were a couple of broken-down English lushes, who ran a seedy saloon within walking distance of Cabo Azul. I don't remember ever seeing either of them smile, their hangovers being even more debilitating than my own. In addition to liquor, they served two kinds of grilled sandwiches: cheese or ham and cheese. Ted grilled these in an aluminum contraption that looked like a waffle maker, but somehow the sandwiches never came out really hot, only lukewarm. His patrons, being three sheets to the wind and not exactly of discerning tastes, didn't complain.

What redeemed Ted & Terry's was their lending library of English paperbacks, most in deplorable condition but if you were desperate for reading matter they were the only game in town. Their most popular American author was Ross MacDonald, whose dark mysteries and brooding private eye Lew Archer made me even more depressed than I already was, what with Juan Lozano pressuring me to marry him and my drinking getting worse by the minute. Then when I least expected it, Joan was back accompanied by her toy poodle, Coco, who had made the airplane trip smuggled inside her shoulder bag. I dislike small overbred dogs in general and I disliked Coco in particular as he was a hyperactive animal, constantly yapping and jumping around, unable to sit still or keep still for more than five minutes, but since Joan adored him there was nothing to do about it. She said that Bela would be coming over as soon as he finished revisions for *Oil*, assuming he lived that long.

"His editor at William Morrow has driven him around the bend," she explained. "He calls Bela at all hours of the day and night with ideas for more revisions. It's a nightmare."

"Why doesn't Bela tell the jerk to knock it off?"

"He feels too intimidated. He thinks that because this book is going to be published in hardcover rather than the usual schlocky paperback original, his editor knows what he's talking about."

"I doubt it."

"You try telling Bela that."

I could see there was no point in pursuing it. "When do you expect him?"

"I'm not sure, but he's definitely coming which means that after all these years of an on-again, off-again romance we're going to be together at last."

"Congratulations. I know how long you've waited for this." While I felt happy for her, I was thinking that the condo would be too small for the three of us. Correction, the four of us now that Coco was on board. What should I do? To leave for London as soon as possible seemed like the obvious answer, except for one problem. Since we didn't have a telephone, I couldn't call the airline for a reservation but had to go into Alicante and do it in person. This might not seem like such a big deal as the bus to Alicante stopped right in front of our door, but because of a raging hangover every morning I found it difficult to go any farther than the bathroom. In fact I found it impossible. The thought of getting dressed, getting on a bus, doing what needed to be done at the airline and getting on another bus back to Campello struck me as daunting as if I were expected to redesign the Sistine Chapel. That's how serious my drinking had become. And yet every night before going to bed, I resolved that in the morning I would stop acting like an idiot and hop on that damn bus. Then when morning rolled around, I would pour some rum into my coffee and another twenty-four hours would be shot to hell.

"I can't seem to get my act together," I told Joan after weeks of inebriation and inactivity had passed. "I don't know what's wrong with me."

"I do." By now she was fed up. "It's called BOOZE."

While I agreed that that accounted for most of my shilly-shallying, I realized I didn't want to leave Campello now that summer had come to the Costa Blanca. The days were warm and sunny, the nights balmy, and the beach literally a stone's throw away from us. It seemed a shame to exchange that for a flat in rainy London, well, at least until the fall. On the other hand I knew that with Bela's imminent arrival, I couldn't continue living at Joan's and that was when inspiration struck. Why not buy my own condo in Cabo Azul? Not only could I afford it, but best of all I wouldn't have to go to Alicante to do it.

No sooner had I arrived at this brilliant solution than I remembered Pessy, an irritating German woman who owned a condo that was for sale, three floors below Joan. We had met her at the *portero*'s grocery store where she was haggling over the price of a can of sardines. Upon exchanging names, she smiled too brightly and said, "Let's go have a nice cup of coffee?" It was a suggestion she would repeat in the weeks ahead with robot-like regularity in a shrill, high-pitched voice that made every sentence she uttered sound like a question. There was something inherently unpleasant about Pessy, untrustworthy, dishonest, her only saving grace being the ability to speak English and after months of listening to nothing but Spanish, Joan and I were prepared to make allowances.

However after a few "nice cups of coffee," we decided we couldn't stand the grinning idiot and went out of our way to avoid her. Now I found myself ringing her doorbell at nine in the morning, my head pounding from too many gin and tonics the night before. Never one to beat around the bush, the minute she opened the door, I said, "I want to buy your condo. How much are you asking?" Although startled (it had been on the market for quite some time), she quickly rallied and flashed that obnoxious smile. "Let's go have a nice cup of coffee?"

In the end, I bought it for thirteen thousand five hundred dollars, which was a fair price at the time and a ridiculously low one when Franco died a few years later and Spain entered the real world. Pessy's condo was not only larger than Joan's, but being a corner unit it had a terrace that ran around the side of the building and commanded a truly spectacular view of the Mediterranean, especially at night when I used to sit out there and gaze at the darkened sea illuminated only by an occasional flash from a fishing boat.

"I guess this means you're not going to London," Juan Lozano said happily, having misgauged the situation.

"Of course I'm going. The condo hasn't changed anything. When I get tired of London, I'll come back here. And vice versa."

"Just like that?"

"Yes, just like that. What's the problem?"

"We must end our relationship. I don't want to be your Spanish lover who you squeeze in when you get tired of your English lover."

"I'm sorry you feel that way, Juan."

He regarded me cynically. "Are you?"

The night before I was due to take possession of my new home, I had a sudden premonition that Pessy was going to try and abscond with all the sheets, pillowcases and blankets that were part of the deal.

"Where is this premonition coming from?" Joan asked.

"My subconscious. Let's go stop her in her tracks."

"What if you're wrong?"

"I'm not wrong." I wasn't. When I asked to see these items, Pessy blanched and pretended she couldn't remember where she had put them. "I know where you put them," I said, pointing to her luggage that was piled up in a corner of the living room. "You've stolen them, you miserable thief."

She vehemently denied it, but when she couldn't show me even one sheet I began screaming at the top of my lungs, threatening her with torture and disfigurement if she didn't produce them. Stunned by my outburst, she caved in and there they were all neatly ironed and folded, nestled into a large brown suitcase. After I transferred everything to a duffle bag I had brought along, Joan and I left.

"At least she didn't say, 'Let's go have a nice cup of coffee?'" Joan said.

My break with Juan Lozano now complete, I spent a lonely boozy summer in my new digs which I had fixed up to the best of my demented ability. Joan seemed glad to be rid of me (who can blame her?) and although we shared an occasional dinner, I was more alone than ever before and as a result, drinking even more heavily. With nobody around to criticize my intake, it had accelerated to an alarming degree, isolation always having that effect on me. The weeks passed in a blurry haze of gin, rum, wine and maudlin self-pity as I incoherently wondered why I was so unhappy when everything on the outside was going so well. That everything on the inside had fallen to pieces because I couldn't stop drinking somehow failed to register. In those years, I attributed eighty percent of my depression to life's travails and twenty percent to alcohol. Later when I learned more about the disease, I reversed the ratio.

One of the worst side effects of my drinking was paranoia and that summer in Cabo Azul it became especially bad. Sometimes I didn't leave the premises for days on end, making do with canned goods and rotgut wine from the *portero*'s grocery store, unable to face a world I perceived as seething with hostility. The more I holed up and drank, the more paranoid and unhappy I became. It was a vicious no-win cycle, my plans to move to London having taken on a remote dreamlike quality by then. For anyone who's not an alcoholic, the solution to stop drinking may seem crystal clear but to an alcoholic it's unacceptable. Instead of viewing alcohol as my enemy, I saw it as my friend and ally feeling that without it I would go to pieces altogether. The idea of a sober life was horrifying. How would I shield myself from all the slings and arrows? How would I get through the day without something to kill the pain? That the pain was caused primarily by what was in my glass rather than in my head again failed to register.

Every once in a while I tried to cut back, but my efforts were largely defeated by the amount of free time I had on my hands. Although I had turned the extra bedroom into an office, I couldn't write a word and blamed it on my surroundings. I had never been productive in beautiful, serene settings. I needed noise, activity, some kind of external energy to get me going. In that case what the hell was I doing in Campello, I asked myself? And why didn't I get out? But how could I get out if I was unable to go to Alicante and make a plane reservation? Was I destined to be trapped in Cabo Azul forever? It began to strike me as a distinct possibility and I often saw myself as an old woman, gray-haired and stooped, telling anyone who would listen that I hadn't left Cabo Azul for the last forty years.

Strange as it may sound, I just couldn't work up the gumption to get on that bus.

The only constructive thing I did during this dismal period was to peruse London travel guides and try to figure out where to make a hotel reservation, my hope being that with a firm commitment perhaps I would finally pull myself together and take off for London. The description of one hotel caught my eye. It was called Dolphin Square and sounded ideal in that it offered housekeeping suites complete with kitchenettes and maid service for a reasonable price. Since I didn't have a phone, I wrote a letter and mailed it in the postal box downstairs relieved that I didn't have to leave Cabo Azul to do it. When I stopped off at the *portero*'s for more supplies, her little store was empty and she regarded me sympathetically. I can only imagine what I must have looked like after weeks of drinking. She asked me how I was and in reply I said I wanted to kill myself. As I would later learn, this was not an acceptable statement in a fiercely Catholic country where suicide is considered a mortal sin.

"You don't mean that, " she said, horrified.

I nodded. "Yes, I do."

Afterward I found out that as a result of this exchange, she had considered having me committed to the local insane asylum but at the time all she said was, "*La vida es dura, Señora.*" Life is hard, Señora. I thought it interesting that an uneducated peasant woman should understand this simple human fact, while I had always expected life to be a bowl of cherries and I wondered if her attitude was the result of growing up in a country that had been bombed, defeated, and occupied by foreign armies whereas as an American I had escaped those horrors. Later when I moved to London, I discovered that the English shared the *portero*'s outlook, they too being able to reflect upon centuries of bloody carnage and strife. Also since both Spain and England were much older civilizations than America, did that make them wiser in their philosophical outlook?

Then gradually my drinking began to abate and I began to spend long hours at the beach getting suntanned (we didn't know it was unhealthy), and wading into the rocky sea to swim. In order not to cut my feet on the ubiquitous jagged rocks, I had bought a pair of the clear plastic sandals that were sold in every shop in town and worn by every person who ventured into this part of the Mediterranean. In Spain, it is believed that the sea cures all ills. It certainly seemed to cure mine and before long I was feeling healthier than I had in months. Every morning when I woke up instead of putting rum in my coffee, I would don my bathing suit and get my beach paraphernalia together, looking forward to the restorative day ahead. I think that the soporific effect of the sun improved the quality of my nightly sleep and immersing myself in the sea soothed my anxious soul. As a Pisces, water has always worked wonders for me.

When I received a confirming letter from Dolphin Square, I felt elated as I mailed them a check for one month's rent for a suite in their main building, Rodney House. I said I would be arriving the second week in September and if there was any problem, to let me know immediately. After two weeks had passed without a word from them, I took the bus into Alicante one morning and made a plane reservation for London. One way. By then it was almost the end of August and although I knew I would return to Cabo Azul at some point, I had a hunch it might not be for quite a while.

"I can't believe you're actually leaving," Joan said, upset because Bela was still stuck in New York doing more revisions on *Oil*. "I was afraid you would drink yourself to death and we'd have to bury you in the Campello cemetery."

Later that evening she, Coco and I went to dinner at La Querencia, Spaniards not only allowing dogs in their restaurants but giving them bowls of water and treating them with affection. Joan said she was going back to New York around the same time that I was going to London since Bela needed her more than ever now that his demanding editor showed no signs of letting up on him. "When I come back here, I assure you that Bela will be with me," she added. "As for you and me, Joyce, I wonder when we'll see each other again."

"I would have thought you'd seen enough of me by now."

"Not when you're sober."

We then nostalgically reviewed everything that had happened to us since we sailed from New York on the *Raffaelo*, unable to believe that it had only been five months ago. It felt like a lifetime.

"There were days when I wanted to kill you because of the drinking," Joan admitted. "But I forgive you, Joyce."

"Well, I don't forgive *you* and I never will."

"Me?" She looked startled. "What did I do?"

"My, how quickly we forget. Maria Montez! The souks! The medina! Arab decadence! Thanks to you, I never got to see Tangier, you bitch."

Then we hugged and said goodbye.

London: 1973

DURING THE YEARS I lived in London, I moved five times but mostly I lived in Dolphin Square. Actually three of those moves took place within this same unique apartment-hotel complex, which is a world unto itself. Situated near the Thames on over an acre of land previously owned by the Duke of Westminster, Dolphin Square was built in 1937 and built so sturdily that its basement provided the perfect bomb shelter when the Luftwaffe struck the city a few years later.

For a long time Dolphin Square had enjoyed the reputation of being the largest block of flats on the Continent. Grouped around beds of beautiful flower gardens, the thirteen massive red brick buildings, each named after a British admiral, had housed a wide variety of tenants: movie stars, call girls, spies, racing car drivers, kept women, playwrights, titled aristocrats, foreign dignitaries, Members of Parliament and, during the Second World War, General Charles de Gaulle himself. While it was rumored that every man in London over the age of twenty-five had had sex in Dolphin Square at least once, all I know for a fact is that in the early Sixties the popular complex made the headlines on two lurid occasions.

The first time was due to a scandal involving Conservative MP John Profumo, which brought down the MacMillan government when Security Services learned that his call girl playmate, Christine Keeler, was also sleeping with a Soviet naval attaché in Keyes House. The second scandal featured Admiralty clerk turned espionage agent, William Vassall, whose rolls of film were confiscated from a custom-built bookcase in Hood House. Who could top that for sheer glamour and intrigue?

My initial accommodation, a studio-cum-kitchenette in Rodney House (the main building) was so tiny that I could barely turn around and most of my clothes remained packed in suitcases due to the insufficient closet space. Although I pleaded with Management for a larger flat, nothing was available just then and I was urged to be patient. Try as I did to follow their advice, I was miserable in such constricting quarters and before long fell under the spell of an American copywriter whom I had met on a blind date. When Alan implored me to move in with him, I don't think I would have agreed if I weren't so unhappy with my Dolphin Square digs. Or maybe I would have regardless, Alan being a very compelling character.

He was smart, intense, attractive in an offbeat way, and imbued with a zany sense of humor which always wins the day with me. Later I realized I should have stayed put at Dolphin Square and waited it out because at first glance I disliked Alan's neighborhood (shleppy West Hempstead) and equally disliked his flat with its tacky furniture and yellowing bluebird wallpaper. However feeling lonely in a foreign country and claustrophobic at Dolphin Square, I was vulnerable to the passionate appeal of a fellow New Yorker.

At first living with Alan was fun. We ran around a lot, went out to dinner, to the theatre, to movies in the West End. I got to know some of his friends whom I liked. We gave a few dinner parties. I ever tried to spruce up his apartment but since it came fully-furnished, there wasn't much I could do to make it more attractive. Alan seemed oblivious to his dreary surroundings and after a while I noticed that he was coming home later and later from the office, spending less and less time with me. When I confronted him about this, he lost his temper and shrieked at the top of his lungs for me to stop harassing him. I had never heard a man raise his voice to such a deafening degree and started to shake uncontrollably. After he stormed out muttering to himself, I ran a hot bath and tried to calm down but I soon discovered that he was a thwarted novelist and jealous of my publishing history. When I happened to mention that I had had six novels published, he turned the color of steamed eggplant and didn't talk to me for days.

Instead of trying to deal with our problems in a constructive way, I began to drink too much which by then was how I dealt with everything. Alan put up with it for a while before taking action. "I'm going to South Africa on business tomorrow," he coolly announced one Sunday afternoon. "I'll be gone for ten days. Don't be here when I get back."

I was dumbstruck. "What do you mean?"

"What does it sound like? Move out, Joyce."

I couldn't believe this was happening to me and my fury knew no bounds. "I just figured out why you look shorter on weekends," I said, freshening my gin and tonic. "It's because when you go to work, you wear boots with heels."

"I'm serious, Joyce."

"So am I, Alan. On weekends, you wear sneakers." I pointed to his feet. "You're easily three inches shorter now than you will be tomorrow morning after you get dressed."

"And you're easily three times drunker and more obnoxious than usual."

I decided to use his kiss-off line ("I'm going to South Africa tomorrow. Don't be here when I get back.") in a future book when the plot called for a rejection of the most ignominious nature. It helped me not to dissolve in tears or kill the insensitive son of a bitch. The next day in a fit of crazed spite, I went to an estate agent and rented the biggest, most attractive maisonette I could afford. In the early Seventies rents were dirt cheap in London, but would sky-rocket when Harold Wilson's Labor Party won the next election. The maisonette was in a neighborhood that Alan liked (Belsize Park), God knows why, and took up three floors, had four bedrooms and a kitchen-dining room of ballroom proportions, making Alan's flat look dwarfish by comparison. Secretly, insanely, I hoped that when he returned from South Africa and saw my new palatial surroundings, he would repent and come live with me.

Later I wondered why the hell I wanted him back. Was it hurt pride? The fear of abandonment? The refusal to face yet another failed relationship? Was it love? Was I nuts or just lonely? Who knows? It didn't matter since Alan had found a new girlfriend in South Africa, a young Canadian whom he moved into his West Hampstead flat with typical lightning speed. When I got him on the phone, he hung up as soon as he realized it was me. Talk about humiliation.

I spent the next year utterly miserable as I ran up and down my triplex wondering what to do with all that space. In desperation I invited a series of friends and acquaintances to come stay with me, hoping they would help ward of the loneliness, but while everyone was kind and supportive they failed to fill the void. At my wits end and fearing a nervous breakdown, I started a new novel called *Getting Away With Murder*. It was published a few years later, but to my disappointment the title was changed to *The Crazy Lovers*. This book had an extremely complicated plot that required all my concentration, which was good as it kept me occupied all day long, yet by nightfall I wanted someone special to share the evening hours with and there wasn't anyone. The loneliness began to accelerate and depression set in.

With the departure of my last house guest, a young Dutchman who ate apples non-stop (seeds, core, and all) I realized that like Alan, the maisonette had been another mistake. While its attractiveness was indisputable, so was its isolation. I was too far away from central London and too cut off from any conceivable social life. The solution seemed clear and in October 1975, I moved back to good old Dolphin Square. This time Management gave me a one-bedroom flat that was decorated in strident burgundy and faced a noisy boys' school. The din was like nothing I had ever heard and in order to write or hear myself think, at least on weekdays, I bought a pair of ear defenders at a gunsmith shop on Bond Street. These contraptions are what target practice people wear to keep from going deaf and they obliterated about eighty percent of the uproar. Unfortunately they were very heavy and I wound up with a headache if I kept them on for any length of time. Since it was impossible to write with a pounding head, I would periodically hightail it to the shopping arcade downstairs.

Dolphin Square had thought of almost every convenience for its tenants (only a post office and shoemaker were missing), meaning that nearly all practical needs could be met without leaving the premises. Not only was there a small but well-stocked supermarket, a butcher, greengrocer, stationery store, an off-license (English for liquor store), but a hairdresser as well. And for diversion, there was a swimming pool with a sculpted brass dolphin, its head rearing out of a large scallop shell, a restaurant overlooking the pool, squash courts, a pub, saunas, a coffee shop, and not least of all a bar.

The bar at Dolphin Square, I would soon learn, was famous throughout London for its ambience of adulterous liaisons, shady deals, and madcap drinking reminiscent of the Twenties. Not only do the English seem to have no guilt about boozing it up, they consider it their birthright. Just so long as a person is properly dressed, courteous and vertical, she can drink herself into oblivion without arousing any criticism. Some days I did just that and some days I settled for a few glasses of white wine. It was on one of those more moderate occasions that I met Dickie Carmichael.

Having finished my grocery shopping in the arcade, I stopped off at the bar before going upstairs to work some more on my new book. Because of licensing laws at the time, all drinking establishments in the U.K. had to close for a few hours at three p.m. sharp and it was almost that when Dickie walked in and took the barstool next to mine. As our eyes met, I felt I wasn't ready for another affair not having completely recovered from Alan's rejection, and yet I knew that the longer I protected myself from involvement the harder it would be to ever trust a man again. Besides, unlike Alan, Dickie was more or less my physical type. He was fair-haired with blue eyes and a straight nose (shades of both my husbands), or as a friend once put it, "Joyce, why are you always attracted to men who would look good in a Nazi uniform?"

Since most of the people at the bar at Dolphin Square knew each other, an outsider's arrival invariably elicited a reaction from the habitués. In Dickie's case, the reaction was quite extreme. I saw blonde, mink-coated Beth Harding give me a sharp look of caution. I saw Susan Dale raise her eyebrows suspiciously. I saw Laura Ashland purse her aristocratic lips and turn away from Dickie. I wondered whether he had had an affair with all of them because he seemed to telegraph sex. It was nothing he actually did, it just oozed out of him. Tall, husky, and built like a football player he, had a dimple in his chin and a very seductive smile. I was finishing my white wine when he asked if he could buy me another before the bar closed.

"I've never known a man who couldn't." It was my campy Tallulah Bankhead takeoff that made me sound a lot more confident than I felt. John Norbury, the bartender, who had a mental dossier on all patrons glanced as me as if to say, "Don't get involved with this one.'" I couldn't imagine what Dickie had done to provoke such mass distrust.

"To Dolphin Square," Dickie said, as we clicked glasses. "Do you come here often?"

"As it happens, I live here. And you?"

"I haven't been by in some time, but I can see that nothing much has changed." He waved to Beth Harding who didn't wave back. "Same lovely clientele."

"I meant where do you live?"

"Earl's Court."

Definitely not a good address, seedy, with lots of SRO accommodations. I couldn't imagine what a person with Dickie's stamp of private schools and upper-class breeding was doing there, but experience had taught me not to ask too many personal questions, at least not at first. The natives didn't appreciate it.

"Closing time, ladies and gentlemen," John Norbury soon announced, throwing another admonitory glance my way. "Drink up, folks. The bar is closing."

Dickie polished off his neat whiskey. "Can I persuade you to have lunch with me?" he asked.

"Thanks, but I'm not hungry. I had a late breakfast."

He looked disappointed. "Bloody shame."

"Yes, it is."

"Well then, Joyce?"

We were reluctant to part, sensing a relationship was in the offing. My intuition said it wouldn't be a serious one and I wouldn't fall in love with Dickie or get hurt. Sex with no strings. It wasn't the kind of relationship I usually sought, but after the debacle with Alan it was the only kind I felt equipped to handle.

"Why don't you come upstairs and I'll fix you a drink?" I suggested, taking the plunge.

He flashed that smile. "Love to."

While he was settling the tab with John, I went to get the grocery packages I had stashed in a corner of the bar. Beth Harding hurried up behind me. She was wearing a kerchief tied in the style of Queen Elizabeth, as usual. "Watch out for that bloke." Her tone was urgent, conspiratorial. "He's nothing but trouble."

"Why? What's wrong with him?"

"He pinches stuff. Hide your jewelry!"

"I don't have jewelry worth pinching. It's all junk."

"You have credit cards, don't you? Put them somewhere safe. Take my advice, Joyce, he's a lowdown no-good bugger."

Beth was a plump attractive blonde, who rarely evinced interest in anything or anyone other than the married Welshman who was footing her bills and I felt surprised that she would care what happened to me. "You don't know Dickie like we do," she went on. "I refer to Susan, Laura, and myself."

The three witches. "I'll be careful, Beth. Thanks for the tip."

"If you have any Georgian silver, hide it!"

"Only two candlesticks."

Her face flooded with alarm. "Don't let Dickie get his greedy little hands on them or you'll never see them again."

I wanted to say I was kidding about the candlesticks, but knowing how seriously the English regarded the possession of Georgian silver I buttoned my lip.

I wasn't surprised when Dickie turned out to be an accomplished, imaginative, and satisfying lover. It was almost as though he had to be to compensate for all the things that were missing between us: shared interests, compatible personalities, not to mention the ability to make each other happy or miserable. My hunch was that Dickie not only had had a lot of experience with women, but was altogether amoral. If it was warm, he'd fuck it. Probably if it was cold, too. For once, that was okay in my book since it absolved me of any emotional responsibilities. Dickie may have been my type physically, but he wasn't my type in any other way and I sensed I wasn't his either.

"How about if I moved in?" he asked when we were sitting up in bed, smoking the clichéd cigarette.

"In where?"

"Here. With you."

"Why would you want to do that?"

"I like you, Joyce."

It hardly seemed like a compelling reason but maybe despite his toney accent and well-heeled façade, he was broke. It would be very Henry Jamesian. So I asked.

"Yes. Broke. Quite. But don't think I'm a freeloader who would move in with just anyone. As I said, I genuinely like you." He flushed with embarrassment. "Besides, I'm looking for work. Hope to find something soon."

"What is it that you do?"

"Matter of fact, I've done a number of things. Racing car driver. Golf pro. Worked in sales for Seagram's when I lived in the States." He tapped his head. "Damned good salesman, too."

"What were you doing in America?"

A gray cast came over his otherwise cheerful features. "Was married when I lived in Kentucky. Divorced now. Bloody bitch, my ex, don't miss her at all. It's my daughter, Angela." Suddenly tears began to roll down his cheeks. "Miss her more than I can say. She's five years old, an adorable child, very bright." He repeated these qualities as though trying to assure himself they were true. "Five years old. Adorable. Bright."

"She sounds—"

I was cut off by the sound of deep racking sobs. Dickie Carmichael had collapsed in tears of remorse, moaning and shaking all over. It was quite a sight seeing this large mound of masculinity crying his heart out, especially since Englishmen were even less prone to displays of emotion than their American counterparts. When I complimented him on being more demonstrative than his countrymen, he said he wasn't English but Scottish and the Celts were an emotional breed. "Born outside of Edinburgh in a town called Gullane," he added.

"Then why do you speak with an English accent?"

"Had an English nanny and was sent to English schools." He smiled through his tears at my ignorance. "It's only the working-class Scots who sound like they have hot potatoes in their mouth."

"Are you sorry your daughter will be educated in America?"

"Wouldn't give two figs where she was educated just so long as I could see her occasionally. Love her so bloody much. But the ex wants me out of the picture, is trying to deny me visiting privileges, hates my guts in actual fact." A fit of paralyzing grief attacked him again. "She accused me of being a waster, a remittance man, an unprincipled gigolo. Said I was a bad influence on my darling Angela. Not true of course. I come from a distinguished family. My father was an admiral in the British navy and my grandfather invented the Carmichael topcoat. See what I mean?"

"Not exactly."

"The ex accused me falsely. Lies, all lies. She wants to separate me from my daughter, the scheming cow. Wouldn't be surprised if she plans to remarry and present Angela with a new daddy. Over my dead body!"

I wondered if he had forgotten about moving in with me.

"It's why I can't live alone," he blubbered. "Can't deal with the grief by myself. It's too debilitating. Thought I was going to blow my brains out living alone in Earl's Court." His sensitivity made him seem even more attractive than when he only had good manners and a dimple in his chin going for him. "You're saving my life, Joyce. You know that, don't you?"

"I hope you don't have a lot of clothes. The closets here leave a great deal to be desired."

"Not to worry, love. Most of my things are in Scotland."

Later I was surprised that I let Dickie Carmichael zero in on me after such a short acquaintance, but perhaps it was a last-ditch attempt to banish Alan's ghost for once and all. I still thought of Alan, haunted by the cruel way he ended our affair. ("I'm going to South Africa tomorrow. Don't be here when I get back.") To celebrate Dickie becoming my roommate, we went to Inigo Jones for steak tartare washed down with champagne and later made love for hours. I considered it a good sign that Dickie wanted to in spite of his pressing problems. I also considered it a good sign that he had picked up the restaurant tab without hesitation. Maybe he wasn't as broke as he claimed.

Just as I was starting to feel optimistic about our living arrangement, Dickie rolled over in bed and his side of the mattress sank almost to the floor in hypnotic slow motion, while I, at half his weight, found myself suspended in mid-air. We must have balanced things out earlier by being together in the middle whereas now it was like being on a seesaw.

"Bloody strange bed," Dickie said, as startled as I by this lopsided development.

"It must be the springs, they're not individually coiled. I used to work for Simmons, the Beautyrest firm. Something like this could never happen on a Beautyrest mattress."

It was little consolation and we stared bleakly at each other. "Goodnight, love." Dickie waved up at me. "Sleep tight. By the way, I don't snore."

Still I knew that if he rolled over or got up to go to the bathroom, I would be awake like a shot. I can live without food if I have to, without exercise, even without fresh air, but the one thing I can't live without and still function, especially if I'm in the middle of a book, is sleep. The lack of it makes me irritable, short tempered and totally crazy, which was how I felt the next day after a night of Dickie's restless tossing and turning.

I must have dozed off near morning because the next thing I knew, a blast from the boy's school across the street pierced the silence. Cursing I put on my ear defenders, the sight of which made Dickie break into a wide grin.

"I have to wear them or I'll go berserk," I said as he trailed me into the kitchenette. "Do you drink coffee or tea?" I read his lips. "Coffee. Good. So do I." I got out the can of coffee, cream, bread, butter, jam. "Would you like some toast?"

He nodded, still grinning, and I realized how idiotic I must have looked with ear defenders sitting on top of hair that hadn't yet been combed and was uncontrollable by nature. To add to the dismal picture, I had unthinkingly donned an old robe that I should have thrown out years ago. "Excuse my appearance," I said. "I'm not used to being with anyone in the morning." On weekdays Alan would have left for work by the time I got up and on weekends he disappeared for a long walk, first thing. Upon his return, he used to entertain me with a comical rundown of his perambulatory observations. His delivery was razor sharp, his viewpoint very much on my own wacky wavelength. Here we go again, folks. When would I resign myself to the fact that I had lost Alan and it was probably a blessing in disguise? Even my therapist regarded our breakup as the best thing that could have happened to me. Coincidentally he had treated Alan's ex-wife and regarded Alan as a poor excuse for a human being.

"What is it about this man you miss so much?" Dr. Watkins had asked.

"His sense of humor."

"Watch Monty Python."

The advice fell on deaf ears. "Alan was the funniest man I have ever been involved with. I can forgive a lot of things when someone is that funny. He used to have me in stitches."

"What about his temper tantrums? Did they have you in stitches, too?"

"Every clown has a dark underside. It comes with the territory. Besides, I only saw him lose his temper three times."

"Yes, but as I recall those three times were close together and happened near the end of your relationship. Don't you realize that his hatred of women was finally surfacing and accelerating?"

"You think Alan hated women?"

"Decidedly," Dr. Watkins said. "In my opinion, a misogynist like Alan could never make a woman happy. You're well rid of him, Joyce...."

"Your tea kettle is whistling," Dickie said.

He removed my ear defenders to tell me this and I wondered why he didn't turn the kettle off himself. I wondered why Dr. Watkins thought a man could make me happy. Didn't he know that happiness was supposed to come from within? Or hadn't that piece of psychological wisdom caught up with the English yet?

When I ran into Beth Harding at the bar later that day, Dickie having mysteriously gone off to Harrod's, she asked if he had disappeared with anything expensive of mine. "He hasn't disappeared at all. He's moved in," I said. "Why are you looking at me like that?"

"Give me your credit cards this instant." She grabbed my purse and rifled through it. "Where are they? I'm doing this for your own protection, Joyce. He stole Laura Ashland's pavé diamond earrings, you know."

"I don't believe it."

"Ask Laura."

"How did she say it happened?"

"Dickie stayed over at her flat one night and when he left in the morning, so did her earrings."

"She probably misplaced them. You're accusing the wrong man."

Beth batted her innocent baby blue eyes. "Why would we want to do a nasty thing like that?"

"I have no idea, but I'm certain that Dickie isn't a jewel thief."

"Don't romanticize the bugger. He would steal the gold out of your fillings, if you had any." Her hand was still extended. "You'll thank me for this."

I doubted it but with my brain fried from lack of sleep, I gave her credit cards for Lloyd's, Harrod's, John Lewis, American Express, Peter Robinson and Barclaycard. "What if I should need them?" I asked as she snapped her purse shut. "What do I do then?"

"Pay cash until the son of a bitch moves out." She headed for the door. "Hide your fur coats!"

I turned to John, the bartender. "Dickie's moved in with me and Beth is holding my credit cards for the duration. Do you think I've made a mistake?"

John poured me a large glass of white wine. "A double mistake."

When I went upstairs, my phone was ringing. It was Katie, my only American friend left in London. "Who's Dickie Carmichael?" she asked. "He just called me."

I had met Katie years ago at the Hotel Chelsea just before her fourth marriage to a pal of mine, composer George Kleinsinger. Although their union disintegrated soon afterward, Katie and I remained close. She was now married for the fifth time to a handsome Englishman who worked as an underwriter at Lloyd's. "Why did Dickie call you?" I said. I had no recollection of giving him her number. "What did he want?"

"He told me that he intends to take very good care of you. He said he's living with you." She sounded impressed. "Is that true?"

"Yes, he moved in yesterday. He's a sensational lover."

"No kidding? Tell me more."

"He's totally depraved. He'd screw a snake."

"That's not very flattering to you, is it?"

"I'm not in this for flattery. I'm trying to get over Alan."

"I thought you got over him ages ago. What does Dickie do for a living?"

"He's a jewel thief," I wanted to say. "He doesn't do anything at the moment. He's unemployed."

"Maybe he has family money. He certainly has a super accent."

"He claims that his money is tied up in some trust fund that he might never be able to collect unless he lives to a hundred and four. Where was he when he called you?"

"In Harrod's food halls, shopping for your dinner. You're having cold roast pheasant tonight. His call was a good sign, Joyce, it shows that he feels guilty about being short of funds. It shows he has a conscience." Katie adopted her businesslike tone. "This isn't America. It's very hard to get a job here. The unemployment rate is staggering. Dickie's heart may be in the right place. Give him a chance."

I thought of Beth Harding and my confiscated credit cards. I thought of John Norbury's warning. "The denizens of Dolphin Square are convinced he's a rotter."

"Don't listen to them. Trust funds were meant to be broken." Katie was the recipient of one herself, so presumably she knew what she was talking about. "The important thing is that Dickie *has* a trust fund, which is more than can be said for weekly-paycheck Alan."

"Alan had other qualities. He was smart and funny."

"I'll take a trust fund any day in the week."

Although there was no way any of us could have foreseen it at the time, ten years later Katie and Dickie got married. Then they got divorced. It was a bitter breakup with each one running the other down and telling me how lucky they were to be free of each other. Miraculously I managed to stay friends with both of them.

Dickie was surprised to learn what my occupation was. At first when I said "writer" he made the same mistake as many of his countrymen. He thought I said "rider" and his face lit up. "Well done, you!"

"I'm afraid you don't understand," I quickly explained. "I'm a WRITER."

After living in London for several years, I knew that only two things impressed the English: being a member of the peerage and being able to ride well. All else paled by comparison and that included talent, money, power, ambition, genius, generosity, decency, kindness and good will toward men. A person could have pulled himself up from the depths of abject poverty and gone on to form an empire, given employment to millions, donated to worthy charities, protected the environment, retained the respect of business associates, the love of an adoring wife and children, been awarded the Nobel Peace Prize, but he would not have been as revered as the sixth lord of Gloucestershire who had won the Whitbread Trophy at Badminton. "I'm sorry to disappoint you, Dickie, but I'm a novelist. I've never been on a horse in my life."

His smile faded and his tone became polite. "Are you writing anything at the moment?"

"Yes, my seventh book."

He acknowledged the Smith-Corona on my desk with a nod. "Ah, so that's what the machine is for."

"It's for torture. This is the hardest book I've ever attempted. It spans thirty years and jumps around all over the world, describing backgrounds and activities that in some cases I have no firsthand knowledge of. I think I've bitten off more than I can chew."

"Why don't you put it away for a while? No point in driving yourself up a wall, is there?"

"I have a contract, a deadline to meet, and I'm going to be late as it is. I not only can't put this book away, I have to speed it up or I'm in serious trouble."

Dickie smiled the way one would smile at a child who had invented an imaginary playmate. He assumed that I was valiantly compiling some fictional fragments that I hoped would *become* a book some day in the distant future, but he did not for one second believe this was how I made a living. The reason for his skepticism had to do with the impoverished state of English publishing, which afforded almost no writer a decent wage, and it also had to do with the way female writers were perceived in the U.K. Either they were married to wealthy men and divided their time between a flat in Belgravia and a country house in Surrey, or they taught at a dreary girls' school while trying to write at night in a bedsit in Maida Vale, or else they were brainy lesbians of independent means toiling away in the family manse in Hampstead.

Dickie wasn't the first dubious Brit I had run across. My friend Gunther Schmeidler who lived in Beatty House, told me that no one at the bar at Dolphin Square believed I supported myself by my writing. They thought I was financially secure because my father was president of Chase Manhattan Bank. I never found out how that crazy rumor got started, but it gave me a good laugh. Apparently it hadn't occurred to the English that the American publishing scene was considerably more affluent than their own.

"What's your book about?" Dickie asked, trying to humor me.

"A brother and sister who run around the world murdering people for money, so they can be together."

He perked up. "Are we talking incest here?"

"Yes, the brother-sister variety. It's quite poignant, really. I have a hunch a lot more of it goes on than people suspect."

"Were you attracted to your brother?"

"I don't have a brother. I'm an only child. Probably nobody except an only child would attempt this kind of book. It's a fantasy, you see."

"Quite. "

If I wanted to pass myself off as a successful novelist, it was fine with Dickie Carmichael. Not only did the English treat lying as an acceptable way of life, my circumstances made it all right. Obviously I had money from somewhere or I wouldn't be living in a fully-serviced flat at Dolphin Square with a closetful of evening clothes, fur coats, and no sign of gainful employment. Next to being listed in Debrett's and being able to ride well, what the English respect most is the ability to indulge one's eccentricities. The work ethic does not score high in England. Growing zinnias scores higher.

"Look at this," I said to Dickie, pointing to a map of St. Moritz that I had thumbtacked to the wall next to my desk. "The protagonists in my book have just gone to St. Moritz on holiday and I'm stuck. Not only can't I ski, I can't figure out the various slopes and how to get to them. This map is no help at all. Do you, by some remote chance, ski?"

He beamed. "It was a lucky day when you met me, Joyce. In addition to being an expert skier, I know St. Moritz like the back of my hand. I used to go there every winter, even did the famed Cresta Run in my time."

"Really? That's fantastic." He could have stolen Laura Ashland's pavé diamond earrings and swindled every woman in Dolphin Square for all I cared. "The characters I'm writing about are experienced skiers. Which slope would they choose?"

"Piz Nair. It's just under ten thousand feet. They would ski down the east side to Marguns."

"And then?"

"They would probably ski to Trais Fluors, then to Marguns again. I guess you've never been to St. Moritz."

"Only for ten days trying to do research. I took a few ski lessons with an ex-Nazi who kept screaming at me to keep my knees together." I shuddered at the memory. "What would my characters do after Marguns?"

"If it were around lunchtime, which I assume it is since they would be sure to get an early start, they would take the lift to Corviglia and have lunch at the private club."

"Wait a minute." I was writing everything down. "How would they get to Piz Nair to start with?"

"That depends. Are they staying at a hotel or a private chalet?"

"Hotel."

"They would take the hotel's helicopter to Corviglia and from there a cable car to Piz Nair. It's about a two-hour trip."

"Would you circle all these places on the map and draw a red line connecting them? That will make it easier when I write the actual scene."

"Happy to oblige." After he finished, he grinned. "I can't believe you would go to St. Moritz to learn how to ski. It's no place for a novice. It has the highest slopes in Europe and as I'm sure you discovered, it's no picnic getting to them."

He didn't have to remind me of the long early morning trek involving icy paths and two tram cars. I used to feel worn out by the time I reached the slopes and had nothing but admiration for the vigorous elderly couples I saw who took this routine in stride. They were like another race—ruddy-faced, steely-eyed, bursting with vitality in their durable anoraks and woolen caps.

"I didn't go there to learn how to ski," I said. "Don't you understand? I was doing research for my book."

Since Dickie didn't buy my being a professional writer, he discreetly circumvented this remark. "Where did you stay?"

"At the Monopole. Everyone else there was coupled. I was the only person by myself. If not for the Italian waiter and Swiss barmaid, I wouldn't have had a soul to talk to. I was miserable for the entire ten days."

"You should have stayed at the Steffani, it's much livelier. What time of year was this?"

"February, high season. The prices were unbelievable and so was the conspicuous consumption. I have never seen so many sables and ermines in my life, ditto for rubies and emeralds, Piguets and Rolexes. With everyone trying to upstage everyone else, I knew I couldn't compete so I wore a five dollar Mickey Mouse watch. You might say it created quite a stir."

Dickie was amused. "I'll bet it did."

"Nobody could figure out why I was waltzing around with such a cheap wristwatch if I could afford St. Moritz in high season. Even the owner of the Palace Hotel became bug-eyed staring at Mickey Mouse, but he didn't say a word. Nobody did. Rich people can be very corny."

"They probably thought you were an eccentric millionaire."

"That's what I was hoping they would think."

Dickie was looking at me in a new way. I wondered if it was what *he* thought.

Every morning after breakfast, he would bathe and put on his best dark suit, starched white shirt, conservative tie, and announce that he was going job-hunting. Since I had no reason to doubt him, I always wished him luck and then settled down to work on the St. Moritz section of my book, which thanks to his help was turning into a far more manageable project than I had anticipated. In fact I couldn't get over how lucky I was to have met someone who knew so much about skiing and St. Moritz just when I needed the information so badly. It made me wonder if the breakup with Alan wasn't for the best because had we stayed together, I never would have hooked up with Dickie. Despite all of my moaning and groaning about the romantic disasters that continued to befall me, I knew if I were ever forced to choose I would take a good book over a good relationship any day in the week.

When Dickie returned late in the afternoon, he would tell me that he hadn't found a job. I would console him, pour us both a glass of wine and bombard him with more questions about skiing, ski clothes, après ski activities and the daredevil Cresta Run, which I had decided to incorporate into my book. Why not, since I had the voice of authority sitting right beside me? Dickie was only too happy to answer all my questions perhaps because after hours of rejection at employment agencies, he liked feeling useful and important. I hung on his every word, made copious notes, and thanked him repeatedly for his assistance.

Some evenings I cooked dinner and some evenings we ate downstairs in the restaurant overlooking the swimming pool. The food wasn't very good, but the Art Deco ambience more than compensated for it and I pretended it was the Thirties when Dolphin Square had been built. The word "service" really meant something back then. Mail was delivered six times a day, errand boys walked the residents' dogs, and a florist came to one's flat to personally supervise the arrangement of fresh flowers. "It must have been wonderful to be rich in England before World War II changed everything," I said to Dickie. "Those times will never come again."

"I would settle for being rich in England right now. I would even settle for being gainfully employed."

"You'll find something eventually. Don't give up."

"It's hard not to when you've been rejected for every job you apply for."

"I can imagine," I said, automatically.

"Can you?"

I realized I couldn't. We were a mismatched couple, a self-made American woman of humble origins and a born-to-the-manor but penniless Scot. Other than sex and St. Moritz, we had little in common and dinner conversation was often a strain. Having prevailed upon Beth Harding to return my credit cards, I usually charged our meals although sometimes Dickie insisted upon paying. It seemed to be a point of pride with him. Then we would adjourn to the bar for cognac, which would have been a pleasant interlude if the regulars hadn't treated Dickie with such disdain. In his zeal to be accepted, he made matters worse.

"My grandfather invented the Carmichael topcoat, you know," he would announce as an opening gambit.

Aside from the fact that no one had solicited this information, the English are repelled by any kind of boasting or bragging whether it be justified or not. Modesty and self-effacement are what win the day with these people and it seemed strange that I should know this and Dickie shouldn't. As he went on to extol the virtues of his father, the Admiral who died young, I saw John Norbury roll his eyes in disgust while several of the regulars regarded me sympathetically. The more cold and rejecting they became, the harder Dickie tried to worm his way into their good graces and one night the spectacle was so painful that I insisted we leave.

"I don't understand what they have against me," he grumbled

once we were in my flat. "I've never done anything to any of them."

"That's not the way I hear it." I figured it was time to tell him the rumors. "Beth Harding says you stole Laura Ashland's pavé diamond earrings."

"That's preposterous." Astonishment shone in his eyes. If it was an act, it was a good one. "Why would she make up a story like that? It's utter rubbish. I'm not a thief. You believe me, don't you, Joyce?"

"Of course I do." Actually part of me believed him and another part believed Beth Harding.

"I'm going to have a little talk with Beth first thing tomorrow. Set her straight, the stupid lying cow." He sounded determined. "Can't let people go around denigrating one's character for no good reason. Bloody unfair is what it is."

"I'm glad you feel that way."

"How did you think I'd feel?" He eyed me indignantly. "Bloody vicious accusation to make about an innocent man. Bloody spiteful, too, just because I wouldn't tumble into the kip with her. Not my cup of tea, that blowsy milkmaid type, never could be."

"Are you saying that Beth made a pass at you and when you turned her down, she concocted this lie?"

"Bloody well looks like it is all I can conclude."

That put a different light on the situation, assuming he was telling the truth. "Why didn't you say so before?" I asked.

"Didn't know about the accusations before. Didn't put two and two together until just now." It made sense, but a few days later I found out that he hadn't confronted Beth. When I asked him why not, he said, "Decided not to lower myself to the level of that stupid bloody cow."

"That's it? That's your explanation?"

He flushed. "Wouldn't do any good. She would only stick to her guns. I would never be able to budge her, not in a million years."

No wonder he couldn't get a job. He lacked self-confidence, assertiveness. He was going to let Beth get away with it without a fight. Even if her story was true, he should have faced her and denied it. *Especially* if it were true. Alan would have denied it, but Alan had New York street smarts having grown up fighting for what he wanted. Dickie had grown up thinking it would be handed to him. Nothing kills romance faster than pity and my mind was already jumping ahead to what would happen once I finished the St. Moritz section. I wouldn't need Dickie's help with the next section, which was set in London. Would I still need or want him? Probably not and I hoped that by then, he wouldn't want me either so the break could be a clean one—and lessen my guilt.

What surprised me was that without love, shared activities, and compelling conversation (a real turn-on for me), the sex had remained so consistently spectacular. I give most of the credit to Dickie because no matter what unpleasantness had taken place during the day, he managed to put it aside in the evening and turn his energies into satisfying the two of us. No effort seemed too great for him, no activity too bizarre.

Once we picked up a girl, brought her back to my flat, and proceeded to have a three-way romp. I'm not ashamed to admit I enjoyed it, yet I doubt I would have done it with any other man. It seemed perfectly natural with Dickie and after he put her in a cab, we spent hours rehashing the event, delighted by our impetuousness. I had the feeling that unlike a lot of men, Dickie genuinely appreciated women and wanted to please them. He certainly wanted to please me and he succeeded. One day he went to a sex shop in Victoria and came back with a vibrator, which he taught me how to use. I didn't like it as much as I liked Dickie and threw it away after we broke up, but at the time I accepted it as a new toy.

I was trying to make sex compensate for all the other qualities that were missing in our relationship, primarily a future. The lack of one made our post-coital happiness short-lived. One minute we would be lying in bed feeling warm and contented, the next minute he would begin moaning about his daughter, Angela. As soon as he did that, my thoughts turned to Alan and the wound that hadn't healed. I envied Dickie the ability to verbalize his grief and wished

I could, too, but I had never mentioned Alan to him and didn't feel this was the right time to start.

"I can't face the future without my darling Angela," Dickie would cry, having moved over to his side of the mattress that now veered toward the floor. "I wouldn't want to go on living if I thought I would never see her again."

"Maybe your ex-wife will relent and give you visiting privileges." Maybe if I asked, that's what Alan's new Canadian girlfriend would give me.

"Angela sent me a birthday card last year, saying how much she loved and missed her daddy. Wanted to know when we were going to be together again." His words were choked with emotion and his shoulders heaved. "What could I tell her? It's up to your rotten bitch of a mother?"

"Your ex-wife shouldn't keep you away from your daughter." Unless she had reasons that he hadn't mentioned. "Angela is your child, after all. You're bound by blood ties."

Alan and I were bound by nothing. It was such a dismal thought that it made me want him more than ever. Imagining I could get over one man who obsessed me by using a second man who didn't had been one of my goofiest mistakes. Live and learn? Sure. Swell. I'll know better next time, folks. At least I would know enough to choose someone with more serene sleeping habits than Dickie. Thanks to his constant tossing and turning I hadn't gotten a good night's sleep since he moved in.

"I never should have married Angela's mother," he moaned. "I don't know what I ever saw in that mean-spirited bitch."

As he wept uncontrollably, I pondered the sleepless night ahead. When morning came I felt like telling him to pack his bags and go back to Earl's Court, but knew I would regret it the minute I sat down at the typewriter. Dickie was better than a hundred reference books and a thousand maps, he was a walking encyclopedia of St. Moritz and I couldn't afford to get rid of him—at least not just yet. If that sounds selfish and conniving, it was but since he wasn't acting out of romantic conviction either, I didn't feel so bad. He had moved in with me for practical financial reasons of his own and I wanted him to stay for practical financial reasons of my own. I guess you could say that in the final analysis, our relationship was a two-way hustle.

What saved us from becoming hard-nosed or callous was that we really liked each other, while remaining totally mystified by each other. Even though Dickie had been married to an American, most of his romantic experiences were with Englishwomen and he seemed startled by my behavior. For instance, one Sunday afternoon we were drinking at the bar at Dolphin Square when an African king swept in with three of his bodyguard entourage, all of them big heavyset men wearing dark suits. The king himself wore a long leopardskin caftan, a leopardskin pillbox hat, a silk crimson cloak flung over his shoulders and tan ropy sandals on his feet. He sat down next to me and proceeded to try to chat me up.

"Hello, young lady. I am King Nubuku of Lagos, Nigeria. And who might you be?"

Not being in an especially friendly mood that day, I said, "Fuck off, king."

Dickie gasped and later admitted he was afraid the bodyguards were going to kill him on the spot for letting me insult their royal leader. I don't remember sharing his fear, but that may have been because I had too much to drink and was feeling no pain. Also as an American, royalty didn't impress me to the degree that it impressed Dickie who was born in a country ruled by a monarchy, albeit a constitutional one. In years to come after Dickie and I remained friends, he would occasionally remind me of the incident at the bar, laughing about it in retrospect, but still visibly impressed. "Joyce, you told a king to fuck off! I will never forget it as long as I live!"

For my part, I was used to American men like Alan with their compulsive ambitions and recognizable goals, not much different from my own. While I realized that the punitive tax structure in the U.K. had killed off many people's incentive, I knew I could never become used to men like Dickie whose attitude toward work was so phlegmatic. Had he railed against Inland Revenue, expressed the desire to emigrate to the United States or Australia where there was more opportunity, had he become indignant about the economic decline of the British Empire, I would have felt more of an affinity with him.

But Dickie didn't do any of those things and gradually I began to see why. He didn't share the American middle-class obsession with getting ahead. Having been born into the privileged British upper-class, he believed he *was* ahead to start with and this nonsense of earning a living was little more than an embarrassment to him, a step down. He once admitted that if he could have things his way, he would spend his time playing golf, lunching at his club, breeding horses and stocking his wine cellar. Those were pursuits worthy of a gentleman, but since this gentleman didn't have any money, on went the dark suit and conservative tie, and out went Dickie to try and find a job. Any kind of job. He didn't care what it was just so long as it covered living expenses until he came into his inheritance, after which he need never work again.

"It's all the Admiral's fault," he added.

"What is?"

"This search of mine for a bloody job. If the old boy had handled his estate properly, I wouldn't be in such a pickle."

"You're a grown man, Dickie. You can't go on blaming your parents for your problems. You have to make your own way in life."

"Easy for you to say. Your father didn't mishandle his estate."

That was the best one yet. "My father didn't have an estate to mishandle. I come from a very poor family. My father was wiped out in the Depression and never recouped his losses. Nobody gave me a dime. Whatever money I have, I earned myself."

He blinked in confusion. "How?"

"How do you think? By writing, of course."

"Sorry, love. I forgot."

It was apparent he would never believe me about that.

One day I broke my morning routine to go visit my friend, Gunther Schmeidler, who lived across the Square in Beatty House. Before Dickie came into my life, Gunther and I had been thick as thieves, talking on the phone at least once a day and visiting back and forth. When he opened the door to his flat, I realized how much I had missed him and how foolish I had been to neglect him. Gunther was his usual dapper self in Harris tweeds and a muted burgundy tie.

"I'm feeling low and need some cheering up," I said. "Have I come to the right place? Is there hope for me?"

Ho ho ho. There is no describing Gunther's booming laugh except to say that it was extremely jovial and made everyone around him want to laugh, too. He gave me a cup of strong coffee and claimed that all of London was depressed due to the economy and the fog, both of which were especially bad that year.

"I don't think that's what's getting me down," I said. "It's Dickie."

"He seems like a decent enough chap." Gunther was the only person in Dolphin Square who hadn't denigrated him. "What's the problem?"

There was no point in detailing the futility of Dickie's aimlessness or the fact that he might be a jewel thief. "Let's just say that it's a difficult relationship."

Gunther nodded, being no stranger to difficult relationships himself. His beautiful young wife had coolly and methodically starved herself to death a few years back by eating five Saltines and drinking a fifth of vodka a day. It took her a year to die, during which time she refused to tell Gunther why she was so intent upon ending her life. "She went to her grave with her secret intact," he had admitted. "Her death will haunt me forever."

Now he asked how my book was coming along and it was a relief to talk to someone who knew me, understood the nature of my work. Gunther and I identified with each other. Neither of us were English, both of us were Jewish and we shared a Germanic heritage. Although he had been born in Berlin and I in New York, our rhythms and lunacies were startlingly similar. I always felt better after talking to him. When he walked me to the lift, he suggested that I give the relationship with Dickie more time. "Maybe that's all it needs, time for you to get to know each other," he said. "You can always break up. That's easy to do."

"You're becoming very wise, Gunther."

Ho ho ho.

As I emerged into the gray light of the Square, I was stunned to see Dickie coming out of Nelson House and, for a moment, thought I was hallucinating. It couldn't be him. He was pounding the West End looking for a job. We met halfway. It was Dickie, all right. "What are you doing here?" I asked, staring at him as if he were a ghost.

"I guess you might as well know the truth." He had turned beet red. "I've been lying to you, Joyce. After the first couple of days, I stopped looking for a job."

"Why? I don't understand. And what were you doing in Nelson House?"

"A stockbroker chap I know has a flat there. Said I could use it while he was at work."

"And that's where you've been all this time? In Nelson House?" I couldn't believe it. "What do you do there?"

"Read the papers, watch the telly. There's no point beating my brains out trying to find employment. Fact is, there's no employment in this city for someone like me. Maybe not in this country."

"Oh, Dickie."

His face was still flushed with embarrassment. "I've been meaning to tell you, but couldn't drum up the nerve."

"I don't know what to say."

"Nothing to be said. It's just one of those things."

I felt incredibly sorry for him. "Where were you headed just now?"

"To lunch. Found an obscure little café not far from here."

"There's no need to hide any longer. Let's go to the restaurant overlooking the swimming pool. Let's be extravagant. My treat. I insist."

We ordered a big meal, washed it down with two bottles of

vintage champagne, laughed at the brass dolphin rearing its head out of a scallop shell, got totally smashed, went upstairs and made love. Without a word, we knew it was over. We also knew we weren't breaking up because he had lied about looking for a job, because I couldn't get a good night's sleep or because he didn't believe I wrote books for a living. While those were contributory factors, the main reason was much more simple. We never should have been together in the first place. We had no common ground.

In the end, Dickie decided to go home to Scotland and live with his widowed mother until he could figure out what to do next. "It hasn't been all bad, has it?" he asked the night before he was due to depart. "I care for you a lot, Joyce, and I'd like to think that you care too."

"I do." Now that he was leaving, I felt a strong surge of affection for him. "You've helped me more than you'll ever know—with my book and also with getting over Alan."

"Who's Alan?"

"The man I was in love with before I met you."

"First I've heard of him."

"One lesson I've learned in England is that a stiff upper lip isn't such a bad idea sometimes. Speaking of which, do you think you could manage not to cry about Angela later tonight? I'm sympathetic to your predicament, but it's a depressing way to end the day."

He flashed that devastating smile. "Agreed."

We got into bed and kissed chastely. Then as he moved over, his side of the mattress sank to the floor. "Sweet dreams," he waved. "Sleep well, love."

"You, too."

I closed my eyes, tired by all that had happened. Tomorrow night Dickie would be gone and I would be sleeping alone. Even though I knew it was for the best, it didn't change my sense of sorrow. Hours later, his voice jolted me awake. "I can't live without my darling, Angela."

As though on cue, Alan's face floated across the pitch black room, his expression intense, sardonic, rejecting. "I'm going to South Africa tomorrow. Don't be here when I get back." I had lied to Dickie about his helping me get over Alan. The wound still festered. And shielded by the night, I succumbed to the luxury of despair, my sobs mingling with Dickie's until we both fell asleep worn out by the specter of irreconcilable loss.

Martha's Vineyard: 1984

As DESPERATELY as I wanted to live in London for the rest of my life, after five years the Home Office (the equivalent of our State Department) caught up with me. I was told that if I wanted to reside in the U.K. I would have to take out residency papers, which would automatically make me subject to the punitive Inland Revenue taxes. I had seen a chart of the tax breakdowns and hard as it was to believe, in my income bracket I would have had to give ninety percent of my earnings to the British government! No wonder so many movie and rock stars had left the country. I later learned that when Margaret Thatcher came to power, I would only have had to shell out fifty percent. Thanks, but no thanks.

The powers that be at the Home Office gave me three months to finish my book and depart. Even though I tried to reason with them, saying not only wasn't I taking anyone's job but was bringing money into the county and should be considered a desirable resident, they wouldn't budge. I cried for two days, finished my book in the three allotted months, and then made arrangements to return to New York in 1978. My farewell to Dolphin Square was very upsetting since I thought of it as home. Several months after Dickie's departure, I had managed to get a lovely quiet flat overlooking the famed gardens. No more noisy boys' school and no more ear defenders to hear myself think. I was so happy my last year in London that to everyone's surprise (including my own), I practically stopped drinking. A couple of glasses of wine a day and that was it. Of course I should have known that any reversal of fortune would make me start boozing it up again and this time in my misery, I became even more frenetic than before. To say that I had to be poured on the plane at Heathrow and off the plane at JFK isn't much of an exaggeration, that's how smashed I was.

Although I dreaded being back in New York, I didn't know where else to go. Not only were my agent, publisher and business manager here, but I had never learned how to drive which made it virtually impossible to consider living in any other part of the country. I realized I had to do two things or I would be stuck in the Big Apple forever. I had to stop drinking *permanently* and I had to get a driver's license. Although it took a lot of hard work and longer than I expected, by the early Eighties I had achieved both goals. Now the only question was, where to go?

Meanwhile I found New York noisier, dirtier, uglier and more alien than ever before. One day while taking a bus down 9th Avenue in the Fifties, I watched a dark-skinned vendor broiling kebabs on a filthy, refuse-littered street and had the eerie sensation of passing through a Middle Eastern slum. Actually I was sick of cities in general. I wanted to hear birds singing when I woke up in the morning rather than the menacing grind of garbage trucks. I wanted to see trees when I looked out the window, not skyscrapers and cement. I wanted to smell clean fresh air. I wanted to walk barefoot in the grass.

I was living in an apartment-hotel on the Upper West side and while my eight-hundred-dollar-a-month digs were considered a great buy in the inflated Manhattan real estate market, I felt suffocated when I came home and double-locked myself in for the night. The kitchenette was a converted broom closet, the bathroom had no window and no exhaust system, the postage stamp living room had no view to speak of, the connecting corridor was long, dark, dreary. My only refuge was the nicely proportioned bedroom, which I had decorated in deepening shades of seafoam green that gave me a sense of wading in a cool clear brook.

I hated to leave that bedroom and couldn't wait to get back to it. Sometimes I cut the evening short so as to dash home to my seafoam bedroom with its expanse of shirred voile curtains and lush leafy plants that fluttered in what appeared to be a natural breeze when I turned on the two fans that I kept plugged in year-round. Every night before going to sleep, I gave the plants a thorough misting in order to keep them healthy during the long, steam-heated winter months. This ritual of mine irritated my one and only suitor, an aeronautical engineer, who I soon realized wanted my undivided attention.

"I've never had to share a woman with a bunch of plants," Steve grumbled. "Making love here is like making love in the Botanical Gardens. All that's missing are the mosquitoes."

"Why do those plants bother you so much?"

"Maybe because you're more attached to them than you are to me."

"That's ridiculous."

"Who are you taking with you when you move? Me or them?"

"I would take you in a heartbeat, but you seem determined to stay in New York."

"Damned right I do and that reminds me. You still haven't said where you're going."

"I haven't figured it out yet."

"What's to figure out? New York is the best." A native son, he had vowed eternal allegiance. "I don't understand why you would even *think* of moving."

"And I don't understand how you can consider staying."

In response he turned over and went to sleep. It irritated me no end that he didn't sit up in bed, smoke the clichéd cigarette, admire my twenty-five thriving plants and admit that the city had become a cesspool. Steve was like a lot of local denizens who managed to delude themselves that nothing had changed. How they accomplished this virtuoso feat was beyond me and I wondered if it wasn't somewhat on the order of the fabled emperor's clothes. I wished New York were the same as it had been back in the Fifties. Hell, I would settle for the late Sixties before everything started going to pieces. Sometimes I dreamed about the city I had known and loved and would never see again.

In 1972 I was a guest on a local Massachusetts radio show to promote my new book, *The Goddess Hangup*, and I predicted that Manhattan would eventually become a city for the very rich and the very poor, and the rich would ride around in bullet-proof cars while the poor took potshots at them. Twelve years later, I wasn't so far off the mark. Middle-class families had been moving away by the hundreds of thousands for a long time, leaving a core of upper-income and lower-income inhabitants who were natural enemies. Here was a recurring image of mine: a long sleek chauffeured limousine is parked outside the Trump Tower awaiting its fashionably dressed and bejeweled owner, as down the street comes a bag lady wheeling all her earthly goods in a shopping cart. It reminded me of the blatant social disparity I remembered seeing on Mexico City's main drag in 1954.

Long after Steve dozed off, his rebuke that I hadn't said where I was going rattled around inside my head. Although I was doing my best to pinpoint a destination, I hadn't succeeded. The only thing I knew for sure was that wherever I moved, it was going to be far from a city and safely within these United States. I had had my fill of foreign lands with their fluctuating exchange rates, punitive residency laws, omnipresent threat of double taxation and diminished chances of gainful employment for non-citizens. Lately those restrictions didn't seem worth the heady sense of freedom I used to feel by living outside my own country. Once in Paris I told a friend that any transgressions occurring abroad didn't "count" the way they did back home and he agreed. Kicking up my heels in a variety of foreign languages had been fun while it lasted, but now I longed to put down roots in good old American soil. I was in the mood to buy property, install a washer-dryer in the basement, plant an herb garden, own a car. For someone who had spent most of her life in serviced apartments, relied on public transportation, and sent her laundry to the dry cleaner, these homey goals seemed exotic.

Over the next few years I became a professional house guest as I hopped around the country, staying with friends in Southern California, Northern Wyoming, rural Oregon and suburban Arizona. After each trip, I listed the pros and cons of the area I had visited and tried to imagine moving there, but to no avail. Southern California was too plastic, Northern Wyoming too culturally bleak, Oregon too depressing, and Arizona too unremittingly cheerful. Ideally I would have liked California's proximity to the ocean, Wyoming's sparse population, Oregon's feisty originality, and Arizona's low humidity all rolled into one neat package.

"You see? I told you there's no place like home," was how Steve would greet my every return. "The trouble with you, Joyce, is you don't know when you're well-off."

"You remind me of the Jews in Germany back in the mid-Thirties."

"Come again?"

"At that time a lot of German Jews refused to believe their world was changing and their lives were in serious jeopardy. It was especially true among the wealthy and prestigious Jewish population in Berlin, who thought of themselves as German first and Jewish afterward. Many of them didn't feel that Hitler posed any threat to them, not even when he broadcast his intentions. Then came Crystal Night and the beginning of the end."

"You consider that an apt analogy" Steve scoffed.

"It's an exaggeration, of course, but there are some similarities. What I don't understand is why, in every age, certain people can see the handwriting on the wall and others can't."

"I'll tell you what I see. A woman who's embarrassed by her compulsively nomadic lifestyle and is grasping at straws to justify it."

Maybe he was right. I once added it up and realized that over the years I had moved twenty-two times within the borough of Manhattan itself. Did I used to like this city? I used to love it, my allegiance having been as fierce and unwavering as Steve's was now. To me New York was the greatest place in the world, not to mention being the center of the universe. Despite the many times I had left to live elsewhere, I always came back to roost and was happy to do so. No, thrilled, because it was mine, my birthright, my heritage, my hometown, mine all mine. And then suddenly, or gradually, or however it happened, it wasn't and, even worse, would never be again.

What's more, I didn't know who was responsible for the city's downfall. Who should I blame? The landlords? Real estate developers? Local government? The drug dealers? Drug addicts? The Yuppies? Donald Trump? Eurotrash? Or were these factions merely players in an inevitable game of destiny. History books are filled with tales of other cities, other countries—entire civilizations, in fact—that enjoyed their day in the sun and then faded from prominence. Why? Did anybody know? Could anybody point to any one thing and say that was what did it? Maybe New York simply had had its day in the sun.

In February 1984, I bought a condominium on Martha's Vineyard. My friend, the much-divorced Katie, who owned property there encouraged me to fly up with her one cold wintry morning and as soon as I saw the terrain, I was hooked. The fact that I didn't know anyone who lived on the Vineyard year-round was somewhat unnerving (Katie only popped in for the occasional weekend and rented out her house the rest of the time), but not unnerving enough to stop me.

Steve was appalled when I told him of my decision. "Have you lost your mind? The Vineyard is a summer resort. Nobody lives there permanently if they can help it. You'll go crazy in the winter. There's nothing to do for excitement. What the hell were you thinking of?"

"Why are you getting so angry?"

"I'm not angry, I'm concerned!" he shouted. "How will you spend your time? Where will you go in the evenings? Do you think the movie houses, art galleries and decent restaurants stay open after Labor Day? Who will you talk to? The birds? There are probably ten people living there on a yearly basis. Carpenters and fishermen."

"Make that approximately fourteen thousand people and what do you have against carpenters and fishermen? Not everyone can be an aeronautical engineer. I might even learn something from these guys."

"Like what? How to build a bookcase out of two-by-fours?"

"I don't know why you consider that so trivial. Maybe it's because those men work with their hands, which makes you think they have no brains."

"You're the one with no brains." He slammed out only to call a little while later. "I'm sorry I blew up, but if I were you I would give this decision of yours some extra-careful consideration. You can always change your mind, you know. How much did you put down on the condo?"

"I have no intention of changing my mind."

"You gave them ten percent, didn't you?"

"That's standard when you sign a purchase and sales agreement."

"I know a good lawyer who can probably help you retrieve some of that money, providing you're willing to admit you've made a mistake. We all make mistakes, Joyce." He was trying to humor me. "The thing to do is be mature and face up to it."

"I haven't made a mistake. You and I simply disagree on this particular subject."

"I should have known something like this would happen when I saw all those plants in your bedroom. I should have realized that you would rather look at trees than go to the ballet. I should have been prepared."

"When was the last time *you* went to the ballet?"

"That's not the point. The point is I know it's there. I can go whenever I choose. What do you plan to do on Martha's Vineyard? Take up square dancing?"

"There are worse activities."

"Such as what? Bird watching? Pottery classes? Looking for arrowheads?"

"Any and all of those."

"Stop kidding yourself. You're a city person, Joyce. You always have been and you always will be. Chances are you don't even know what an arrowhead is."

"Maybe not, but I do know that my hometown has gone to pieces."

"It's easy for you to talk since you can write anywhere. What am I supposed to do? Give up a lucrative profession that I happen to love to move to an island off Massachusetts and become a scallop shucker?"

"Don't be so presumptuous about my work habits. I've written every book in a big city. For all I know, I might get stymied without that frantic urban energy, but I'm willing to chance it. Maybe I'll write a different kind of book or maybe I won't be able to write at all." The idea was terrifying. "Life is about taking risks. It's about moving on if the circumstances warrant it."

"Thank you for those words of wisdom, but Woody Allen and I don't want to move on. We like it here just fine."

Growing up in New York was like growing up anywhere in the United States, I used to think when I was a child. In those pre-television, pre-mass media days there was no way I could have realized how different my urban experience was from small town America. I assumed that everyone lived in a six-story apartment building, took an elevator upstairs and downstairs, called the superintendent for repairs and was conversant with street life. In the Depression years, which was when I grew up, street life had been benign and friendly. On warm afternoons local housewives sat outside on folding chairs, sunning themselves or playing Mah Jong, one eye peeled on their children cavorting nearby. Husbands only seemed to materialize on weekends when they joined their wives and became formal couples, the men in dark suits and ties, the woman in Persian lamb coats and seamed stockings, high heels. They could be seen strolling around the neighborhood arm in arm, on their way to the movies, to visit relatives, to eat chow mein at the Chinese restaurant, to pray at the synagogue on Holy Days.

Everyone walked everywhere. My mother walked to the markets, about eight blocks away, to do her grocery shopping. In the evening, my father walked to the Democratic Club to play pinochle with his buddies. I walked back and forth to both my elementary school and high school for a total of twelve years. I thought nothing of walking to the ice cream parlor after dark to join my friends for a soda. Practically nobody we knew owned a car and neither of my parents ever learned how to drive. When distances became prohibitive, we took the subway or a bus. That's how it was. Since we lived in a rented apartment, we knew nothing about furnaces, washing machines, lawn mowers or mortgage payments. None of us had a clue that compared to the rest of the country, we might as well have been Eskimos living in an igloo.

"I'm moving to Martha's Vineyard," I told everyone who would listen. "What do you think about that?"

"You're not giving up your apartment, are you?" a friend asked, horrified.

"I can't afford to hang onto it and pay a mortgage, too."

"Sublet it."

"What's the point since I never plan to return?"

"That's what you said before you moved to Mexico, Paris, and London."

"Those were only practice moves. This is the real thing."

"You said that before, too. You love to move, Joyce, admit it."

"You're wrong. I hate it, and the older I get, the harder it becomes."

"Then why do you do it so often?"

"I don't hate it once I'm there. I hate the process of moving."

"I would have thought you'd be good at it by now. You've had so much practice."

"Unfortunately that's not the way it works."

While moving is known to be very high on the stress list, I suspect that I react even more intensely than most people. Every time I move, I remember previous times I have moved and become incredibly sad. In fact as soon as I start putting my belongings in packing cartons, I feel engulfed in sadness and find it hard to continue. I can't think of a more forlorn experience than seeing the space where I have lived suddenly stripped bare, reduced to four walls, a floor, a ceiling, all signs of personal occupancy gone. It's as though I were being stripped and reduced. Somebody once told me that I was a born nester who relied too much on my surroundings for identity and security, and I'm afraid it's true.

So is it any wonder that my heart was pounding as I contemplated the Martha's Vineyard move? I was being uprooted from the home I had lived in since my return from London and even though it left a lot to be desired, it didn't necessarily mean that I would like my new home. As a writer, I worked at home and therefore spent more time there than most people. Also I was moving by myself, without companionship or emotional support. Since no one had forced me to move, late at night I had to wonder if I were doing the right thing. Would I be sorry later on? Would I berate myself for not seeing the obvious pitfalls? A year from now, would I wish I had stayed put?

I thought back over all my moves, including those made in foreign countries, and realized that although they totaled thirty-six, regret had set in only once. It happened in the mid-Fifties when I rented a charming skylight flat on Irving Place only to discover on my first night that the water flow was a mere trickle. It took something like an hour and a half to fill up the bathtub. To make matters worse, the landlady, who lived in the building, worked for one of the city's housing authorities and had ascertained that the trickle met legal standards. When I stopped being furious, I decided that the only way out of the mess was to find an unsuspecting tenant to take over my lease. Guilty as it made me feel to foist off the inexcusable water situation on two young innocent girls, I didn't see what choice I had. Then I moved into a rooming house to recuperate from the shock of making two full-scale moves within a one-month period.

"I'm moving to Martha's Vineyard," I told Ernie, an old acquaintance who owned a moving and storage company. "Would you like the job? I'd feel a lot less anxious if you were handling things, especially since I have twenty-five plants that I'm not sure will survive the upheaval."

"Why don't I come over tomorrow and get an idea of how much stuff you have?" Although Ernie and I had been out of touch for a long time, he sounded pleased to hear from me. "Then I can give you a rough estimate of what it will cost."

Ernie had once worked for Ted Peters, who had once worked for me and my first husband when we owned the Hysterical Movers in the early Fifties. Years later when I left my second husband, painter John Hultberg, Ted had bought the Padded Wagon, a landmark Greenwich Village moving company and saved my sanity by offering me gainful employment. I spent six months booking moving jobs, during which time we became romantically involved. In 1961 when Ted and I took off for Mexico (yes, yet another memorable trip south of the border), it was Ernie who sublet my apartment on West 14th Street and agreed to manage the Padded Wagon. Later he told me that he had had a hot affair with a famous folk singer in my bed and every time I saw her on television, I tried to picture them together. Since Ernie was quite short and she was quite tall, it was an amusing image. Ernie had been educated at Princeton and was well versed in a wide variety of subjects, but from the time he discovered the subculture of Village moving companies he became hooked and never worked at anything else.

"Don't worry about your plants," he said the next day after having painstakingly waded through my apartment, peering into clothes closets and inspecting the contents of kitchen cabinets. "What we'll do is wrap each plant in plastic and providing the weather stays above freezing, they should be all right in the van overnight."

"Overnight?" We were back in the living room, watching snow fall on Columbus Avenue. "Why?"

"I checked the ferry schedule to Martha's Vineyard and our best bet is to load your belongings the day before the actual move, then get an early start in the morning. If we tried to do it all the same day, we probably could make a late ferry but by the time my men finished unloading everything, they would be stuck there. That would cost you a hotel bill." He consulted an appointment book. "When do you want to move?"

"Not until April." We were at the tail end of February. "The owner swears my condo will be ready by then."

"What are they doing to it?"

"Everything. The building was recently gutted and rebuilt from scratch. It's an old sea captain's house, three stories high, one unit to a floor. It's charming and conveniently located to boot. I'm only a few blocks from the town, beach and ferry."

"Sounds too good to be true. Did it set you back a bundle?"

"No, compared to New York prices it was a steal." And at least five times larger than my current digs, into which I had crammed too much junk. "I'd like your men to pack for me. I hate dealing with that stuff. It's so emotional."

"No problem." Ernie made a note in his appointment book. "We'll pack you on April first, load you on the second, and move you on the third. If you run into any snags with the completion of the condo, we can always reschedule. At least this way you have a working date."

My hands had become clammy in anticipation of the big move. "That was easy."

"Nervous?"

"Of course, but anxious to get out of here at the same time."

"What made you choose the Vineyard?"

"You mean aside from it being the most beautiful place I've ever seen in my life, as well as being fairly close to New York in case I have to come in to see my agent or publisher?" A glimpse of the New York I used to know suddenly flashed across my mind. "Remember how terrific this city used to be, Ernie? I've been thinking a lot about those days ever since I moved back from London. In fact sometimes it's all I can think of."

"I know what you mean. I feel sorry for the kids who've just arrived and have the current crap to deal with. I often wonder why they stay."

"They have nothing to compare it with. We're spoiled, Ernie. We had the best of this city, so we're not willing to settle for anything less."

"I'm not sure the kids would know the best if it bit them in the nose. All they seem to care about is money and drugs. At least we had ideals. We believed in things like honor."

"It sounds so quaint, doesn't it?"

He didn't appear to hear me. "We even believed in the creative process. Literature with a capital 'L' and art with a capital 'A.' We actually believed that writers and painters could change the world. Back in those days, business was a dirty word and big business was even dirtier. Now all the kids want to do is accumulate as much money as possible, as quickly as possible and stay stoned long enough to enjoy it. I wonder when it all started to go sour."

"When Jack Kennedy was killed. The fact that an American president could be knocked off by some nut with a rifle paved the day for mass disillusionment, fear and cynicism. Then came the assassinations of Bobby Kennedy and Martin Luther King, followed by the Vietnam disaster and the scandal of Watergate. Suddenly nothing seemed sacred any longer."

"I guess it was too much for people to cope with."

"If a country loses its principles, how can individuals be expected to have any? Decadence and greed set in. In my opinion, that's the legacy of the present generation."

"Maybe we're just getting old and crotchety," Ernie said. "Do you think?"

"No. I approve of principles, not to mention romance and love, two subjects about which I've heard very little lately."

"Sometimes I wonder if they're ever coming back," he said. "The other day, my twenty-three-year-old son asked me what to do about a girl he's interested in. Apparently she doesn't know he exists. I told him to send flowers, take her dancing, admit that he cares. At first he thought I was crazy ("Send her *flowers*, Dad?") but after much persuasion, he agreed to give it a try. Guess what happened?"

"She fell into his arms."

"Nope. She said she was allergic to flowers, didn't like to dance, and had the hots for her boss, the CEO of a multi-national corporation. But I'm proud of my son because it made him realize she wasn't the girl for him. 'She has no soul,' he reported. He's decided to become a marine biologist and go to St. Croix where he wants to save the leatherback turtles from extinction, so maybe there's hope yet." Ernie stood up to leave. "Come to think of it, that might explain one of the reasons you chose the Vineyard. I was there not too long ago and had the sense of being back in another era, before fast food chains and shopping malls, before life became so homogenized and computerized."

It was true. Now that he mentioned it, I realized that the Vineyard did seem reminiscent of days gone by. Maybe I wasn't just moving to an island off the coast of Massachusetts, maybe I was moving backward in time—in order to go forward.

"The movers are coming to pack for me on April first," I told Steve that evening. "I know what you're thinking. It's April Fool's day and very appropriate."

"Did I say anything?"

"You didn't have to." We were lying in bed. "Tell me that you'll miss me, at least a little bit."

"I would be a liar if I pretended otherwise, but guess what I won't miss?" He pointed to my array of thriving greenery. "I won't miss making love in a bedroom that looks like Tarzan's Last Stand."

"Ernie promised to wrap the plants in plastic, so they won't freeze." I inched closer to him. "Do you think I'll ever see you again?"

"If you really cared about me, you wouldn't go."

"That's not fair." I refused to let him make me feel guilty. "You can always come and visit. It's only half an hour from LaGuardia."

"There's no point in trying to sustain a long-distance relationship. It never works. When you leave New York, Joyce, that's it."

The reality of the breakup finally hit me. Up until then I had avoided thinking about it because it evoked the memory of too many other breakups, not only both my marriages, but Ted Peters, Juan Lozano in Spain, Alan and Dickie in London, plus some other less significant ones. Just as I had never lived in any one place for very long, I had never remained involved with any one man for very long. When I was younger, it didn't bother me to pick myself up and move on but the older I got the more I let society brainwash me into thinking it was a sign of instability and immaturity. Why had I fallen into that trap? Who was I trying to placate? The truth was that having overcome my initial apprehensions about the Vineyard, I was excited at the thought of being in new surroundings, meeting new people, having new adventures. A brand new chapter in my life was about to unfold and I couldn't wait to embrace it.

For the next month, all I thought about was the move. I flew up to the Vineyard once more to make sure that the flooring had been installed in my condo. (I'd asked for wide pine planks in the living room and foyer, wall-to-wall carpeting in the two bedrooms.) This time I went without Katie who was embroiled in a new romance, anxious to walk around town afterward and savor the atmosphere. My heart was pounding when the nine-seater plane hit the airstrip. It was a damp gray morning, similar to the other time, and as I took a taxi in from the airport I was impressed once again by the astonishing sound of silence. After Manhattan with its incessant grinding noise, I had almost forgotten how peaceful and serene the island was. There was no industry, no pollution, no crowds, no crime to speak of. Vineyard Haven, the town I'd chosen to live in, had been described as the "year-round town," meaning its shops stayed open during the non-tourist months. As my taxi swung up Main Street, I heard a foghorn and could smell the sharp sea air.

"It's two buildings before the library," I told the driver. "The gray house with the widow's walk on top."

"Oh sure, the one that's been renovated."

"I bought the second-floor condo."

"Why did you do that when you could have bought a house probably for a lot less money?"

"I just learned how to drive and with a house, I would need a car right off the bat. This way I can walk most places and ease into driving gradually." I was too embarrassed to admit that I had never driven without the school's instructor seated beside me. "I've never even owned a car."

"You're kidding."

"No, I'm from New York which has a pretty comprehensive public transportation system. A lot of New Yorkers can't drive, you'd be amazed."

"I *am* amazed. I've been behind the wheel since I was twelve." Just as the street turned residential, he pointed to a small park on our right. "The town beach is down there. It's not the greatest beach on this island by any means, but it's within walking distance of you. Or do you plan to rent out your condo in the summer?"

"No, I'm going to live in it. I'm moving here permanently."

"Good for you." He regarded me with fresh interest. "But won't you be bored coming from a big city? There's not much happening on the Vineyard except in July and August."

"I don't see how I could be bored in such beautiful surroundings. Besides, I'm a writer. I'm used to amusing myself."

Seconds later he pulled over to the curb and I got out. The building was exactly as I had remembered it. Plain, simple, unpretentious. I glanced up at the bay window in my kitchen, imagining how it would look filled with some of my plants. Then I walked around to the other side of the building, the alcove off the living room side. That was where I would put my desk and write. I would be facing trees that were bare now, but would soon turn green and leafy. Beyond them lay the harbor. I would catch glimpses of it as I walked to town to do my errands. (It still hadn't registered on me that I would actually be driving before long.) I scanned the street and to my relief, there wasn't a soul in sight. When I had spoken to the real estate agent the previous week, he said the other two condos weren't yet sold and there was no way of knowing how long it would take. As far as I was concerned, it could take forever. I felt like pinching myself. In a few more weeks, this would be home!

"Another writer lives just down the road," the driver said before he took off. "Her last name is Hellman. She's supposed to be pretty famous."

I couldn't believe it. "Lillian Hellman?"

"Beats me." He shrugged. "The only Hellman I know is Hellman's Mayonnaise."

I laughed. What an epitaph for someone with Ms. Hellman's acclaimed literary history! Then I went upstairs to see if my flooring was in.

Soon after I moved to the Vineyard, my publisher rejected the plot outline I had written for my next novel. By "rejected," I mean the advance he offered was a bare fraction of what I was used to getting. He justified his offer by pointing out that my last two books had sold badly. When I said it was a miracle they had sold at all considering the lack of advertising and promotion, he stuck to his guns. Having been with this same publisher for seventeen years, I felt hurt and angry. "It's an insulting, degrading offer," I told my agent. "Please submit the plot outline somewhere else."

I hoped another publisher would see the merits of my proposed book, but no one did and after a while I realized I didn't see much merit in it myself. I had churned out the storyline only because I was used to finishing one book and then after a reasonable interval, starting a new one whether I felt like it or not. Often I didn't feel like it. At least I didn't feel like writing yet another of the zany, sexy, campy creations that had become my trademark, but being paid good money for them I always caved in. Now my gut instinct was telling me to try something new. The only question was *what?*

No matter how hard I concentrated on the problem in the weeks ahead, no ideas came to mind, no inspirations, no revelations. And then I stopped thinking about a new book altogether, forgot about it actually, ceased being obsessed with it. Gone was the compulsion to gulp down a cup of coffee first thing in the morning, head straight for the typewriter and sit there for the next five or six hours, filling up the pages. This sudden loss of interest was unfamiliar and vaguely unsettling. When I looked at my ten published books lined up in the bookcase, it was as though another person had written them. Maybe another person had: the old alcoholic me. Even though I had written the last three while I was getting sober, they reflected the mentality of the person I was when I drank. I was no longer that person.

Over the next few months I stopped feeling guilty about my inability to write and started feeling buoyant about my surroundings. When I looked out the window I saw trees, birds, and an occasional rabbit scurrying across the lawn, rather than the gray cheerless skyscrapers of New York. When I left my building, I didn't have to lock the condo door. (Nobody locked doors or cars on the Vineyard.) As I walked the few blocks to town to do my errands, bracing salt air filled my nostrils. I caught glimpses of the harbor and the small beach where I went to swim in the afternoon. I couldn't believe how spotless and leisurely everything was. People were polite, nobody pushed, nobody shoved, nobody spoke to himself, no bag ladies or derelicts lurking in doorways were anywhere in sight.

Was I on the same planet? It didn't seem possible. In the past I had only felt whole and complete if I were writing a book. Now I started to feel that way all the time. It made me wonder whether my writing days were over and I was supposed to go on to a new field of endeavor, but I couldn't imagine what that field might be. For the moment, I was content to enjoy each lazy languid day. Like a snake shedding old skin, I was shedding workaholic attitudes and learning that it was okay to do nothing more original (at least for a while) than pick up my mail at the post office and read it in a nearby restaurant on the water. I didn't have to buy approval with my books. I was fine as I was. I had always been fine, I just hadn't known it. Every night before I went to sleep, I thanked God for that day's sobriety and for Martha's Vineyard.

Although with the help of a new friend I found a second-hand Audi station wagon not long after settling in, it took a while to get used to driving on hilly, bumpy, winding country roads that required different skills from the flat straight streets of Manhattan with their frequent red lights. It came as a shock to discover that there wasn't one traffic light on the entire island! When you got into your car, you just went, no delays, no time out. As soon as I began feeling comfortable behind the wheel, I began to feel dissatisfied with the location of the condo.

Now that I no longer needed to be within walking distance of town, I wanted more seclusion and privacy. I also wanted some land of my own. I wanted a house in the woods, I realized one day. That I had never owned a house and knew nothing about maintenance or upkeep didn't bother me. I was bothered, however, by the thought of taking out a second mortgage, selling the condo, and facing yet one more move. So bothered that I felt like burying my head in the sand and ignoring this new predicament. If I were drinking, I would have ignored it. Sober, I couldn't. I called the real estate agent who had sold me the condo less than a year before. "I'd like to buy a small inexpensive house surrounded by trees," I told him. "And then I would like to unload the condo. Do you think that's possible?"

To my surprise, he said he might have just the house I described and we arranged for me to look at it the next day. I felt proud of myself. Instead of getting drunk, I had dealt with a problem head on. Maybe this wasn't unusual for most people, but for me it was like walking on the moon. I was lucky in that I found the house I wanted at the price I wanted to pay. I was unlucky in that I hadn't sold the condo by the time I was ready to move. That meant leaving it furnished, so I could rent it during the summer months. Fortunately I had shipped so much furniture from New York that I had enough for both places.

The period that followed was a hectic one. In addition to the chaos of my own move, I was overseeing the condo rental on a week-to-week basis. While this was time-consuming work, I felt restored the minute I returned to my new house nestled in a clearing between oak and pine trees. A small gray-shingled Cape, it stood at the end of a private dirt road off one of the main roads. There were a few other houses scattered about, but they weren't close and nobody drove past me since a thick wooded area lay behind my house. From my deck, all I saw were birds, wildflowers, blueberry patches and an occasional deer. My cat was in heaven and so was I. When fall came, I rented the condo for a year. I wouldn't make much money on it, but it would cover my mortgage and be less of a hassle than dealing with weekly summer people who left the place is such a mess that I had to hire a cleaning woman to come in after they were gone. Eventually I would sell the condo.

The main thing was I had gotten out of a living situation that no longer suited me and into one I loved. I remembered times when I stayed in apartments, cities, and countries I didn't like, with men I didn't like because I was too drunk and too insecure to extricate myself. I thought of the discomfort I had endured, the sense of futility, and all for the next drink. All to keep on drinking and never have to stop. All to keep from feeling the pain. Yet I did feel it. I felt it between drinks, or when I didn't have enough to drink, or when I temporarily sobered up. Then I felt it so much that I went right back to drinking to blot it out again—or try to. And more alcohol was needed each time to do the job right, a lot more. But the job never got done. Not the real job, which was as simple (and complicated) as facing up to what life had dished out and dealing with it to the best of my ability.

When I stopped relying on alcohol to blur my problems, I started relying on myself to resolve them and found I was made of sturdier stuff that I had imagined, which was fortunate since country living seemed filled with surprises. Some of these were irritating (a sudden power failure of indeterminate length), some were startling (a skunk watching me hang out the wash on a clothesline I had rigged up), some were dangerous (the pipe of my wood-burning stove falling off in my hands and flames shooting up to the ceiling), and some were comical (what I thought was an attractive stone sculpture outside my bedroom window turned out to be a huge wasps' nest).

Even after a few years, the charm hadn't disappeared. I still enjoyed finding the first tulip of spring, seeing a buck race across my lawn, feeding cracked corn to the birds, gathering kindling for the stove, walking on a blustery beach in December. I even enjoyed boarding up the windows in preparation for a hurricane or going out at night in a robe and pajamas to sweep falling snow off my car before it froze solid. I liked being exposed to the elements as I never was in New York. I think it's good to know the difference between what exists naturally and what is manmade. In cities we lose sight of these basic differences and, I believe, in the end, of ourselves.

I also discovered something about my love affair with the bottle. Like many mind-altering drugs, alcohol had shown me where I wanted to go but alcohol couldn't get me there. It didn't have the power. I needed sobriety to connect me to stronger forces than my earthbound self. Whether these forces are God or nature is beside the point. Call them what you will. I feel that I instinctively knew I wasn't here alone or by sheer brute chance, but to live my life with as much courage and joy as possible before I returned to where I came from. I think that's really the goal. Addiction brings no joy (oblivion isn't joyful) and certainly requires no courage. Kicking addiction is the first step to plunging into the mysteries of the universe. I never thought I would hear myself say this, but if you stick with it long enough, kicking ends up being the biggest kick of all.

THE END

About the Author

JOYCE ELBERT was born in the Bronx on February 26, 1930, the only child of Melba and Charles Krimmer, an Austrian immigrant whose once-thriving dress manufacturing company went bankrupt during the Great Depression. She attended New York City's Christopher Columbus High School and Hunter College, from which she received a bachelor of arts degree in Journalism in 1952.

In 1958, Elbert was one of the founding editors of the *Provincetown Review*, a literary magazine for which author Norman Mailer served as advisor. Her first novel, the semi-autobiographical *Getting Rid of Richard*, was completed in 1959 although it didn't see publication until 1972. Her 1969 novel, *The Crazy Ladies*, was dubbed "the first really great dirty book" by *Cosmopolitan*. In 1980, more than 5,000,000 copies of her books were in print worldwide, including translations into Spanish, French, German, and Croatian.

Elbert's last published novel, *The Return of the Crazy Ladies*, was released in 1984. She died on May 8, 2009, in Volusia, Florida, of amyotrophic lateral sclerosis (Lou Gehrig's disease), leaving behind at least seven unpublished novels, as well as several short stories and autobiographical essays.

Acknowledgments

Profound thanks are extended to the following for their generous financial support which helped to defray some of this publication's production costs:

Alan J Abrams, Kevin Adams, Rune Andersen,
Dennys Antunish, Thomas Young Barmore Jr,
Tara Barnes, Sam Bertram, L.M. Beuthe,
Brad Bigelow (The Neglected Books Page), Matthew Boe,
Brian R. Boisvert, Ashley Bray, Michael Harry Broder,
David Brownless, Chris Call, Captain Awesome,
Noah Castellanos, Scott Chiddister, Joel Coblentz, K. Coleman,
S Costa, CTH Costas, Parker & Malcolm Curtis, dcmalone,
Edward De Vere, Isaac Ehrlich, Pops Feibel, John Feins,
Fred Filios, Raymond Foye, Elise G., Justin Gallant,
Hugh Geenen, Stephan Glander, GMarkC, Janice Goldblatt,
Linda Gonzales, Kelly Graham, Everett Haagsma, Lesley Hall,
Mahan Harirsaz, Heather Harkins, Aric Herzog,
Morgan Hobbs, Tom Hochman, isaac hoff, Hall Hood,
Lora J Ingram, Erik T Johnson, Fred W Johnson, Alex Juarez,
Rebekah Kass, Stefan Kruger, Kyle, Jamie Lammers,
Gardner Linn, Nick Long, Elizabeth J Maxim, David McCarty,
Jim McElroy, Donald McGowan, Ian McMillan, Jack Mearns,
Jason Miller, mky, Spencer F Montgomery, Moog,
Gregory Moses, Scott Murphy, Matt "Devilboy" Murray,
Clyde Nads, Michael O'Shaughnessy, Andrew Pearson,
Rachel Peterson, Julie Phillips, Stephen Press, Kate R,
Ned Raggett, Judith Redding, Kay Reindl, Robert Riley-Mercado,

George Salis (www.TheCollidescope.com), David W. Sanderson,
Florian Schiffmann, James C. Schoech, Spike Schwab,
Kelly Snyder, Yvonne Solomon, Jared Stearns, K.L. Stokes,
Stephen Michael Tabler, S. W. Thompson, Elisa Townshend,
Alex Traynor, Cato Vandrare, Elizabeth Weitzman, Rachel Wells,
Paulie Wenger, Isaiah Whisner, Charles Wilkins,
Christina Woelke, T.R. Wolfe, Michelle Mae Yee,
The Zemenides Family, and Anonymous

www.ingramcontent.com/pod-product-compliance
Lightning Source LLC
Chambersburg PA
CBHW011150290426
44109CB00025B/2552